Global Activator

Your English, My English, World Englishes!

Tadashi Shiozawa
Gregory A. King

KINSEIDO

Kinseido Publishing Co., Ltd.
3-21 Kanda Jimbo-cho, Chiyoda-ku,
Tokyo 101-0051, Japan

Copyright © 2015 by Tadashi Shiozawa
　　　　　　　　　Gregory A. King

All rights reserved. No part of this publication may be reproduced, stored in a retrieval system, or transmitted, in any form or by any means, electronic, mechanical, photocopying, recording or otherwise, without the prior permission of the publisher.

First published 2015 by Kinseido Publishing Co., Ltd.

Acknowledgment
Design　　　　sein
Illustrations　　Kyoko Ogura

音声ファイル無料ダウンロード

https://www.kinsei-do.co.jp/download/4003

この教科書で 🎧 DL 00 の表示がある箇所の音声は、上記 URL または QR コードにて無料でダウンロードできます。自習用音声としてご活用ください。

▶ PC からのダウンロードをお勧めします。スマートフォンなどでダウンロードされる場合は、ダウンロード前に「解凍アプリ」をインストールしてください。
▶ URL は、検索ボックスではなくアドレスバー (URL 表示欄) に入力してください。
▶ お使いのネットワーク環境によっては、ダウンロードできない場合があります。

🔘 CD 00　左記の表示がある箇所の音声は、教室用 CD (Class Audio CD) に収録されています。

は じ め に

　世界の多様な英語を地域性・社会性の現れた正当な英語として肯定的に認知し、互いに尊重し合うというのが「国際英語論」の基本的な考え方です。*Global Activator* は、この「国際英語論」の考え方を本格的に取り入れた総合英語教材です。ただ、国際英語論は「なまりが強く、誤りが多い英語」を容認するものではありません。あくまで、互いの少しの努力と歩み寄りにより、世界で十分機能する英語を使うべきである、という前提に立ちます。また、英語教育の視点から言えば、まさにそここそを英語学習者の到達目標にすべきであると考えます。その方が心理的な負担が少ないばかりか、世界的な英語使用の現状にも合っているからです。この考え方を延長すれば、日本人ももっと自信を持って日本人英語、突き詰めれば "My English" を使うべきであり、その過程で総合的な英語力を上げればよいと考えることができます。必然的に本書はインタラクション活動が多く、インプットとしては、ネイティブスピーカーの英語を含む、地域性や民族性が現れた様々な英語が一つのモデルとして提示されています。

　もちろん、*Global Activator* は、先行シリーズの *Activator* や *New Activator* と同様に、消極的な英語学習者に「挑戦」します。彼らが本来持っているコミュニケーションへの欲求を「活性化」させ、その楽しさと可能性を実感してもらうことが本書の本来の目的です。学習者たちは、常に「自分たちに関係すること」を英語で話し、聞き、読み、書く（メモを取る）という言語活動に身を置きます。しかも、それぞれの言語活動は、シンプルで有意味性と多様性に富んでいますので、比較的消極的な学習者でも、自然と言語活動に取り組むようになるはずです。

　本書で世界共通語の一つとしての英語を楽しみながら学び、「自分の英語」に自信をつけていただければ幸いです。

著者

Introduction

Global Activator is a multi-skilled, function-situation based textbook wholly written for Japanese college-aged learners of English as a "global language." Throughout the textbook English is treated as a tool for global communication for native AND non-native speakers of English. Learners are constantly encouraged to use their own varieties of English as long as it is intelligible even if they may have a perceived accent or structural mistakes. It is assumed that, by using their own varieties of English, learners will develop confidence and global communication strategies, which will in turn improve their overall English proficiency.

One of the biggest features of ***Global Activator*** is in its recordings. Native speakers of English along with non-native speakers who use their regional/social variety of English participated in the recordings of the model dialogues and listening exercises for every chapter. Learners are provided with ample opportunities to listen to different varieties of English as global communication models. Another feature found in each chapter is the column named "World Englishes," where specific strategies or methods for attitude training are introduced to students so that they can develop confidence in cross-cultural communication using their own varieties of English. In short, *Global Activator* challenges the common problems of the "perfectionistic attitude" of Japanese college students and releasees them from the idea that they have to sound and speak like a native speaker of English.

Global Activator, like its predecessors *Activator* and *New Activator*, also keeps the tradition of challenging "passive learners" and not allowing them to sit quietly and do nothing in class. Task-based, fun and motivating exercises throughout the course with highly relevant topics to the life of Japanese college students will "activate" their desire to communicate in English. Students will experience the pleasure of communication and build confidence in using English in a meaningful way. Non-threatening and highly personalized activities will enable passive learners to use target expressions in meaningful and communicative ways. The learners are assured of leaving the classroom with a sense of achievement and satisfaction.

Suggestions

To make the best use of ***Global Activator***, it is highly recommended that learners work through the activities with a partner. Most activities in this book have been designed to be conducted in pairs or groups so that the students have the opportunity to practice interaction in English during each lesson. With ***Global Activator***, students do most of the talking, not the teacher. Each unit can be completed within a 90-minute lesson; however, depending on the level or creativity of the learners, it could be conducted in two separate lessons. *Global Activator* is designed to be taught by either native or non-native speakers of English. Please make the best use of yourself as a native or non-native teacher. And most importantly, please have fun teaching with *Global Activator*. It is designed for both students and teachers to explore the language in an enjoyable way.

TOPIC QUESTIONS

Each unit starts with a brainstorming introduction exercise with highly personalized questions.

DIALOGUE

Learners practice the first part of the dialogue and replace parts of it to fit their own situation so that the dialogue becomes more meaningful. As a short listening exercise, the rest of the conversation with some surprising conclusions follows. Two sets of conversations are recorded using both a World English model and a standard American English model.

EXPRESSIONS FOR INTERACTION

Several basic target expressions are provided, followed by some controlled and communicative exercises. The type of exercise varies from unit to unit.

WORLD ENGLISHES

An encouraging message regarding the use of English as their own language is provided with a unique strategy training exercise.

LISTENING ACTIVITIES

Learners listen to interviews given to actual users of World Englishes and answer the questions that follow.

READING ACTIVITIES

An interesting and thought-provoking story on the theme of each unit is provided. Learners are NOT expected to understand all of the words or expressions. Comprehension exercises follow each reading.

GLOBAL ACTIVATOR

Highly communicative and interactive (and often open-ended) exercises conclude each unit. Some optional challenging discussion exercises are also provided.

Contents

Unit 1 — *College Life* 2
World Englishes: Japan
Functions: Greetings/Getting to Know Each Other

Unit 2 — *Mobile Phones* 8
World Englishes: England
Functions: Making Appointments/Phone Conversations

Unit 3 — *Movies* 14
World Englishes: India
Functions: Inviting/Accepting and Refusing

Unit 4 — *Dating* 20
World Englishes: Mexico
Functions: Describing Someone

Unit 5 — *International Food* 26
World Englishes: Korea
Functions: Requesting/Restaurant Conversations

Unit 6 — *World Englishes* 32
World Englishes: Singapore
Functions: Asking for Repetition/Clarification

Unit 7 — *Weekends/Vacations* 38
World Englishes: Hong Kong
Functions: Talking about Free Time

Unit 8 — *Music/Songs* 44
World Englishes: USA 1 —African-American English—
Functions: Expressing Likes/Dislikes

Unit 9 — Sports 50
World Englishes: Australia
Functions: Commenting/Expressing Feelings

Unit 10 — Shopping 56
World Englishes: China
Functions: Negotiating/Expressions for Shopping

Unit 11 — Traveling/Studying Overseas 62
World Englishes: USA 2 —Midwestern English—
Functions: Expressions for Traveling

Unit 12 — Festivals/Parties 68
World Englishes: Germany
Functions: Asking Favors/Asking for Permission

Unit 13 — Part-time/Future Jobs 74
World Englishes: Brazil
Functions: Conveying Intentions/Future Plans

Unit 14 — Experiences 80
World Englishes: The Philippines
Functions: Asking for Help/Talking about Experiences

Unit 15 — Cool Japan 86
World Englishes: France
Functions: Giving Suggestions/Opinions

Unit 1

College Life

Functions

Greetings/Getting to Know Each Other

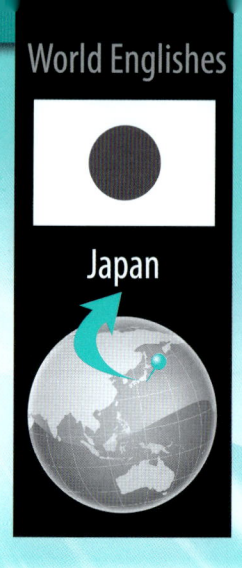

World Englishes

Japan

🌐 TOPIC QUESTIONS

A Fill in the blanks with your own information and practice saying them with a partner. Try to be original and informative.

1. *A:* Where did you go to high school?
   B: I went to _____ High School in _____.

2. *A:* How did you like your high school?
   B: _____. (I loved it / I hated it / It was OK)

3. *A:* What was your favorite subject?
   B: I liked _____ best, but I didn't like _____.

4. *A:* Were you in any school clubs?
   B: Yes, I was in the _____. / No, _____.

5. *A:* Do you live with your family or do you live in an apartment?
   B: I live with _____. / I live alone in a(n) _____ tatami-mat apartment. (six / eight)

6. *A:* How do you come to school?
   B: I _____ to school. (take a train/bus / drive / walk)

B Change roles and ask the same questions. Be sure to ask and answer follow-up questions.

2

Unit 1 College Life

DIALOGUE

🎧 DL 002 ⦿ CD1-02 ● 🇺🇸   🎧 DL 003 ⦿ CD1-03 🇺🇸

A *Listen to the conversation and practice with a partner.*

Mana sees Pat, an international student from the U.S., on campus.

Mana: Hi, <u>Pat</u>. How're you doing?
Pat: <u>Pretty good</u>. Thanks. You?
Mana: <u>Couldn't be better</u>.
Pat: That's good.
Mana: You know what? I just found out that a very close friend of mine is also in our department.
Pat: Let me guess. It's <u>Yumi Miyake, right</u>?
Mana: How did you know that?
Pat: Well, <u>she</u> is my <u>conversation partner</u>. <u>She</u> told me that <u>she</u> went to the same high school with you: <u>Hashima-Kita High School</u>.
Mana: Wow. Did <u>she</u> also tell you that we were even in the same club—<u>band</u>?
Pat: Really? I didn't know that.

B *Replace the underlined words with your own information. Be sure to listen to your partner and change the underlined parts appropriately.*

🎧 DL 004 ⦿ CD1-04 ● 🇯🇵   🎧 DL 005 ⦿ CD1-05 🇺🇸

C *Listen to the rest of the conversation and answer the questions.*

1. What instrument did Mana play in her high school band?

2. Are Mana and Yumi good musicians?

3. What kind of band are they going to form?

4. What are they majoring in?

5. When are they getting together for the first meeting?

3

EXPRESSIONS FOR INTERACTION

A *Practice each dialogue with a partner. Replace the underlined words with your own information.*

Greetings

1. A: Hi, <u>Akira</u>. **How're you doing?**
   B: **<u>Pretty good</u>.**

2. A: **What's up?**
   B: **<u>Not much</u>**. How about you?

Getting to Know Each Other

1. A: **Where did you go to high school?**
   B: I went to <u>Tokyo Minami</u> High School.

2. A: **How do you like school so far?**
   B: Oh, **<u>I love it / I hate it / it's OK</u>**.

B *Fill in the blanks with appropriate words. Practice with a partner.*

1. A: How do you like our department so _____?
   B: Oh, I love it.

2. A: What club were you in when you were in high school?
   B: I was _____ the soccer club.

3. A: How're you doing?
   B: _____ bad at all. In fact I'm doing _____.

4. A: _____ do you come to school?
   B: I usually come to school by train and bus, but sometimes I walk to school from the station.

5. A: What is your major?
   B: I'm majoring _____ economics.

C *Use each of the questions on the next page to start a short conversation. Try to speak for at least 20 seconds. Look at the example and notice how the follow-up questions keep the conversation going.*

> **Example**
>
> A: Where did you go to high school?
> B: I went to Kyoto Nishi High School.
> A: Where is that?
> B: It's near Kyoto University.
> A: Did you like it?
> B: Yes, I really liked my high school. In fact ...

1. Do you have any brothers or sisters?
2. Where are you from?
3. Do you have any hobbies?
4. What classes are you taking here?
5. Are you in any clubs or circles here?
6. Do you live at home with your family or in an apartment by yourself?
7. Was this school your first choice?
8. What would you like to do in the future?
9. Are you happy with your life at school now? Why?/Why not?
10. What do you usually do after school?

WORLD ENGLISHES

Three circles of English

English spoken as a native language is called English in the **Inner Circle**, English spoken as a second language is called English in the **Outer Circle**, and English spoken as a foreign language is called English in the **Expanding Circle**.

Which circle does English spoken in the following countries belong to? Group them.

England, the Philippines, Singapore, Hong Kong, Nigeria, Japan, India, China, Brazil, Australia, France, New Zealand, Bhutan, the U.S.

Inner Circle:
Outer Circle:
Expanding Circle:

🎧 LISTENING ACTIVITIES　　　DL 007　CD1-07

Listen to the interview. Take notes and answer the questions.

Notes

....
....
....

Questions

1. What department is he studying in?
2. Why did he choose the university he attends?
3. What does he like about his school life?
4. What is he most worried about?
5. What would he like to do in the future?

📖 READING ACTIVITIES　　　DL 008　CD1-08

Here is an email that Jack, a new international student to a Japanese university, wrote to his mother back in the U.S.

A *Read the passage and fill in the blanks with the words listed below.*

food	talk	*kaiten-zushi*	outside	make-up
five	90	*hanami*	studying	once

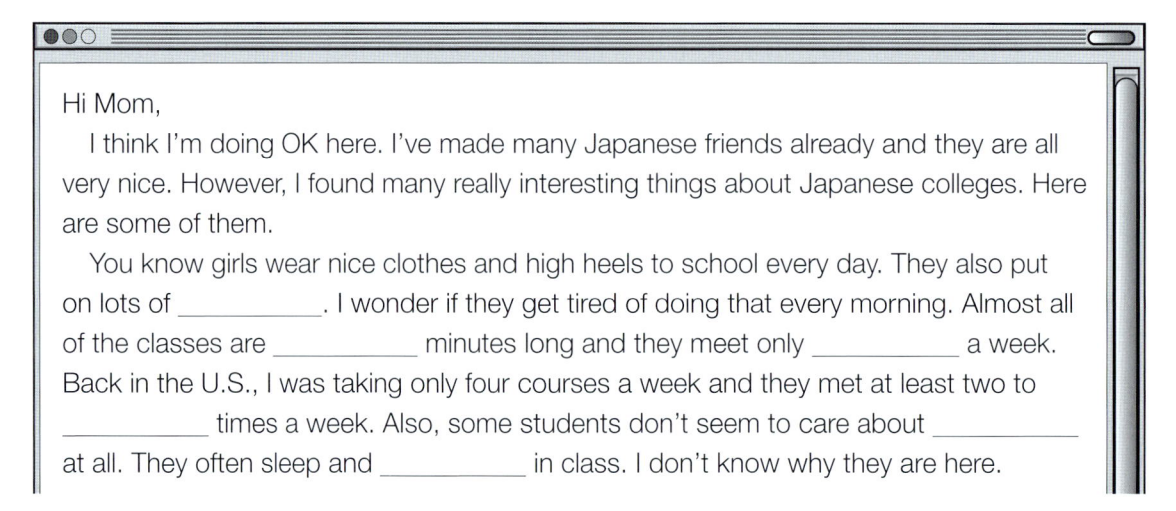

Hi Mom,

　I think I'm doing OK here. I've made many Japanese friends already and they are all very nice. However, I found many really interesting things about Japanese colleges. Here are some of them.

　You know girls wear nice clothes and high heels to school every day. They also put on lots of _____. I wonder if they get tired of doing that every morning. Almost all of the classes are _____ minutes long and they meet only _____ a week. Back in the U.S., I was taking only four courses a week and they met at least two to _____ times a week. Also, some students don't seem to care about _____ at all. They often sleep and _____ in class. I don't know why they are here.

Unit 1 College Life

However, there are lots of things I like. They seem to be extra nice to foreigners. They also try to talk to me in English, which is really nice. The _____ is great here in Japan. I love *takoyaki* (ball-shaped octopus dumplings), _____ (inexpensive sushi that comes to you on plates on a circular conveyer belt), and lots of others. The best thing I like is that we can drink _____. It was really nice to go out and drink under the cherry trees when they were in bloom. They call it _____, which means cherry blossom viewing.

I'll write you more about my life in Japan later.

Love,
Jack

B *(Optional)* **If you were to email your high school friends who are NOT going to college about your college life, what would you tell them? List at least two ideas and discuss them with a partner.**

1. _____
2. _____

GLOBAL ACTIVATOR

A *Move around and find someone who has done the following activities. Write down their names if they say 'Yes.' Do NOT write the same person's name more than once.*

1. Do you like college better than high school? (   )
2. Do you walk to school? (   )
3. Were you in the chorus club in high school? (   )
4. Do you live with your grandparent(s)? (   )
5. Was this school your second choice? (   )
6. Are you happy with your school life? (   )
7. Do you have a scholarship? (   )

B *(Optional)* **Discuss the questions below in a pair or small group.**

- Do you think going to college is a waste of time or is it necessary?
- Do we need to learn a foreign language at the college level? Why?

Unit 2

Mobile Phones

Functions

Making Appointments/Phone Conversations

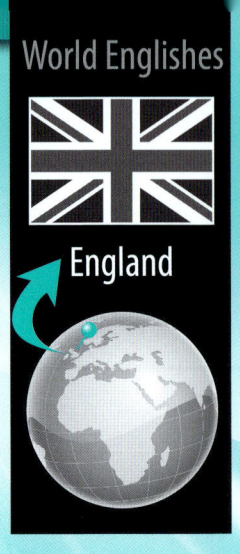

World Englishes

England

TOPIC QUESTIONS

A *Fill in the blanks with your own information and practice saying them with a partner. Try to be original and informative.*

1. A: When did you get your first mobile phone?
   B: When I was _____ years old.

2. A: How often do you use your phone to make calls?
   B: _____. (Rarely / 2-3 times a day / A lot)

3. A: Which do you like better, talking or texting?
   B: I like _____ (talking / texting) better because _____.

4. A: How often do you check your text messages?
   B: _____. (A few times a day / Very often / All the time)

5. A: How much is your average monthly phone bill?
   B: It's about _____ yen.

6. A: May I have your phone number?
   B: Yes, it's _____. / Why do you need it?

B *Change roles and ask the same questions. Be sure to ask and answer follow-up questions.*

Unit 2 Mobile Phones

DIALOGUE 🎧 DL 009 💿 CD1-09   🇬🇧   🎧 DL 010 💿 CD1-10 🇺🇸

A *Listen to the conversation and practice with a partner.*

Erina is making a phone call to Phil, an international student from England.

Erina: Hello, Phil?
Phil: Speaking.
Erina: Hi, Phil. This is Erina.
Phil: Hi, Erina. What's up?
Erina: Well, I'm calling about the interview we set up ….
Phil: Yes. You want to ask me about England for your seminar?
Erina: Right. Can I meet you at McDonald's on campus?
Phil: McDonald's is fine. When?
Erina: How about 4:00 this Friday?
Phil: Sorry, I can't make it. I have class until 4:20.
Erina: OK. Can we meet at 4:30 then?
Phil: 4:30 is fine with me.
Erina: Great. See you then. I really appreciate it.
Phil: No problem. See you at 4:30, on Friday at McDonald's on campus.

B *Replace the underlined words with your own information. Be sure to listen to your partner and change the underlined parts appropriately.*

🎧 DL 011 💿 CD1-11   🇬🇧   🎧 DL 012 💿 CD1-12 🇺🇸

C *Listen to the rest of the conversation and take notes. Where and when are they meeting? What are they doing after the meeting?*

Notes:
....
....
....
....

Where: _____

When: _____

What: _____

9

EXPRESSIONS FOR INTERACTION

A *Practice each dialogue with a partner. Replace the underlined words with your own information.*

Making Appointments

1. A: **Can we meet at** the Softbank shop around 11:00?
   B: **Sorry, can you make it** after school?

2. A: **Are you free** this Saturday evening?
   B: Saturday evening? **Let me check my schedule.**

Telephone Conversations

1. A: **May I speak to** Akira?
   B: **This is he (she). / Speaking.**

2. A: **Can I take a message?**
   B: Yes. **Can you tell** Julian that I'll be late for the meeting?

B *Find the BEST response. Practice asking and answering the questions with a partner.*

1. Do you text?
   a. No, textbooks.   **b.** Speaking.   **c.** I like talking on the phone better.
2. I think you have the wrong number.
   a. Mistake.   **b.** Sorry, what number is this?   **c.** Can I take a message?
3. Can I meet you at your apartment at 9:30?
   a. Yes, I can.   **b.** Turn right at the light.   **c.** How about at 10:00?
4. I'd like to make an appointment to see Dr. Laurence at 5:00.
   a. You can't!   **b.** Good choice.   **c.** Certainly.
5. What can I do for you?
   a. Yes, I'd like to make an appointment for 4:00.
   b. No, you can't.
   c. Yes, can you call me back later?

C *Make appointments on the phone with a partner based on the information given on the next page. Be original and creative.*

Unit 2 Mobile Phones

| Example | information |

A: **lunch, 12:30, cafeteria**
B: **12:30 is too early, change the time**

> A: Hey, you want to have lunch with us today?
> B: Sure. What time?
> A: 12:30, at the school cafeteria.
> B: 12:30 is a little too early. Can you make it 12:45?
> A: No problem. OK, we'll see you at the cafeteria at 12:45.
> B: The cafeteria at 12:45. Great. See you then.

1. A: meet at the airport, 10:00
   B: 10:00 is too late, make it 9:30
2. A: go shopping, this Saturday morning
   B: hate shopping, want to have a barbecue at the river
3. A: go to a DoCoMo shop, this evening, your mobile phone broke
   B: too busy this evening, change the day
4. A: *(Your own question)* _____
   B: *(Your own question)* _____

WORLD ENGLISHES

English speakers in the world

Read the passage and fill in the blanks in the graph with A, B, or C.

It is estimated that over 1.5-2 billion people (The world population is about 7.2billion) can speak English worldwide. According to the British Council, there are (A) 375 million people using English as a second language, whereas (B) 750 million people are using English as a foreign language. The number of native speakers of English is only about (C) 350 million. It seems there are many more non-native speakers of English than native speakers. No wonder there are so many varieties of English today. Who is in the minority here?

23% ( )
52% ( )
25% ( )

Global English speakers in the world

11

LISTENING ACTIVITIES

DL 014　CD1-14

Listen to the interview. Take notes and answer the questions.

Notes

....
....
....

Questions

1. When did he first come to Japan and how long has he been here?
2. Can he live without his mobile phone?
3. Which messaging application does he like most and why?
4. What's the biggest difference between Japanese and British people in the use of mobile phones?
5. What does he think of people using mobile phones on trains?

READING ACTIVITIES

DL 015　CD1-15

Pair up and choose A or B. If you're A, read Passage A aloud. B should close their textbook and take notes. Change roles and do the same for Passage B. Ask at least two questions to each other.

Here is some information about mobile phones around the world.

A: So many people have mobile phones now. There are about 7,200,000,000 people in the world and 6,311,000,000 mobile phones are in active use. In Japan, the number of mobile phone subscribers is about 138,000,000, which is higher than the population of Japan. In China over 1,100,000,000 mobile phones are active now. Some say that the number of people in the world who have mobile phones is higher than those who have access to sanitary toilets.

B: Mobile phones are just like computers these days. In Kenya, you can send money directly to a mobile phone number, and the holder of that mobile phone can go to a nearby kiosk and get the electronic money in cash. Of course you can use mobile phones for texting, taking pictures, recording sounds, listening to music, finding information, playing games, studying English, translating languages, finding directions, reading comics, banking, turning on the TV, and much, much more.

Unit 2 Mobile Phones

Q1. _____

Q2. _____

GLOBAL ACTIVATOR

A *Pair up and complete the dialogue with a partner.*

Sophia, a guest from England, is visiting you on campus. You and your friend want to take her around the neighborhood. On the phone discuss where you should go, what you want to do, what you want to eat, and what she should buy as a souvenir. Also decide where and what time you will meet on campus.

- A: Hello, may I speak to _____?
- B: Speaking.
- A: Oh, hi _____. Sophia is coming to campus at 11:00 tomorrow. We should show her around. Do you have any ideas about where we should take her?
- B: Great. How about _____?
- A: That sounds good. OK, what can we do there?
- B: Well, we can _____.
- A: What do you think we should do for lunch?
- B: Maybe we should take her to (the name of a restaurant near your school).
- A: No, no. That's not Japanese. We should take her to a real Japanese place.
- B: Should we take her to (the name of a restaurant near your school)?
- A: Hey, that's perfect. That's very Japanese.
- B: … and we should take her to _____. She can do some shopping there.
- A: Good idea. What do you think she should buy as a souvenir?
- B: Well, how about _____ or _____?
- A: That sounds great. OK, can we meet sometime before 11:00?
- B: Sure, how about _____ near _____?
- A: OK. Near _____ at _____. See you then.
- B: OK. It's going to be fun.

B *(Optional) Find a new partner and make a similar kind of conversation with your new partner.*

■ This time, you are taking an international guest to any place you like in Japan for two days. You're picking up your friend (your partner) and the international guest in your car at a nearby station. Do not look at the textbook.

13

Unit 3

Movies

Functions

Inviting/Accepting and Refusing

World Englishes

India

TOPIC QUESTIONS

A *Fill in the blanks with your own information and practice saying them with a partner. Try to be original and informative.*

1. *A:* What's the best movie you have ever seen?
   B: The best movie I have ever seen is _____.

2. *A:* How often do you go to the movies?
   B: I (rarely) go to the movies _____. (once a month / once a year)

3. *A:* Who is your favorite actor or actress? Why?
   B: I like _____ best. He/She is so _____.
   (cool / handsome / pretty)

4. *A:* What did you think of (*the name of your favorite movie*)?
   B: Oh, _____. (I loved it / I hated it / it was OK) because _____.

5. *A:* Have you seen any good movies recently?
   B: Yeah, I saw _____ _____ _____ ago.

6. *A:* What kind of movies do you like?
   B: I like _____.
   (comedies / science fiction / romance / dramas / action / mysteries)

B *Change roles and ask the same questions. Be sure to ask and answer follow-up questions.*

Unit 3 Movies

DIALOGUE

DL 016 CD1-16 ● 🇮🇳 DL 017 CD1-17 🇺🇸

A *Listen to the conversation and practice with a partner.*

Shota asks Aditi, an international student from India, out to a movie.

Shota: Hey, you want to go see a movie this weekend?
Aditi: Maybe. It depends on the movie.
Shota: Well, a new movie called <u>Dancing Maharajas III</u> just came out.
Aditi: That's from <u>India</u>.
Shota: Yes, and I thought you might like it.
Aditi: Yeah, I love <u>Dancing Maharajas</u>.
Shota: So, you want to come?
Aditi: Sure, I'd be glad to.
Shota: Great! So, does <u>Saturday</u> evening work for you?
Aditi: It sure does. Where and what time?
Shota: Let's meet at <u>Hachiko</u> at <u>4:00</u>.
Aditi: <u>Hachiko at 4:00</u>. Gotcha.

B *Replace the underlined words with your own information. Be sure to listen to your partner and change the underlined parts appropriately.*

DL 018 CD1-18 ● 🇮🇳 DL 019 CD1-19 🇺🇸

C *Listen to the rest of the conversation and answer the questions.*

1. What is Shota doing with Indian movies?

2. Why do Indian movies always have dance scenes?

3. Are music and dances more important than stories in Indian movies?

4. Do they have bed scenes in Indian movies?

5. According to Aditi, are Indian dances in the movies sexy?

15

EXPRESSIONS FOR INTERACTION

A *Practice each dialogue with a partner. Replace the underlined words with your own information.*

Inviting Someone/Accepting and Refusing Invitations

1. A: **Would you like to** go see a movie this weekend?
   B: **I'd love to.** Thank you for asking.

2. A: **Do you want to** go out drinking with us tonight?
   B: Um, **let me think about it**.

3. A: **Why don't we** go bowling after school today?
   B: **Sure.** Can you wait at the school gate around 5:00?

4. A: **Are you interested in** going for a drive this Saturday?
   B: **I wish I could but** I've already made plans.

B *Accept or refuse the invitations using the phrases below and ask one extra question.*

Example

A: **Do you want to** go drinking this Friday evening?
B: **Sure. / Why not? / Where do you want to go?**
   I wish I could, but I have to do my homework.

A: **How about** Takohachi near the station?
B: **No, let's try** Coopers, the British place.

1. How would you like to see a movie with me this weekend?

2. Hey, do you want to have lunch? I'm really hungry.

3. Are you interested in seeing a movie tonight?

4. Tomorrow is my birthday. Do you want to come to my party?

5. Why don't we play soccer this afternoon?

6. *(Your own question)* _____?

C *Invite your partner to the following events.*

Your partner needs to refuse the invitation first. Then you have to somehow convince your partner to come. Finally, your partner should agree.

1. Going to India together during your next vacation

2. Going to see a new film from Bhutan

3. Making a movie in English for a school festival

DL 021 ~ 023   CD1-21 ~ CD1-23

WORLD ENGLISHES

Accent is OK

Do not hesitate to use your own variety of English, which is your Japanese English. Everybody has an accent. Accents are OK as long as they are intelligible.

Listen to the three sets of passages spoken by three different speakers. Rate the speakers on it if it is easy or difficult to understand them. Circle your answer and write your reasons. Discuss your answers with your classmates.

Passage 1. (easy   OK   difficult   very difficult)
Reason: _____

Passage 2. (easy   OK   difficult   very difficult)
Reason: _____

Passage 3. (easy   OK   difficult   very difficult)
Reason: _____

LISTENING ACTIVITIES

Listen to the interview. Take notes and answer the questions.

Notes

Questions

1. Where in India is this student from?
2. Why did she come to the U.S.?
3. How often does she watch movies in the U.S.?
4. What does she like about Bollywood movies?
5. What is the name of the Bollywood movie she recommended?

READING ACTIVITIES

Read the passage about Bollywood movies and answer the questions.

Where do you think the world's movie capital is? Hollywood? Wrong! It's Bollywood. Bollywood is the nickname for the Indian film industry located in Bombay (now known as Mumbai.) As many as 1,000 films are made each year in Mumbai, whereas only 700 films are made in Hollywood. A government-owned studio facility known as "Film City" is the center of the industry.

Here are some of the interesting figures for Bollywood movies. Fourteen million Indians go to the movies on a daily basis and pay a typical Indian's day's wages (U.S. $1-3) to see a film. Movies are three to four hours long; include dozens of songs and dances (sometimes over 100 dancers), top stars, lots of action, and always a happy ending.

Since India is a country of sixteen official languages and a total of twenty-four languages spoken by over a million people each, some films are made in English, Hindi, Tamil, and Bengali among others.

Why are Bollywood movies so popular? People say it's because they are colorful, packed with singing, dancing, and have loads of costume changes, which help you escape from the real world.

Unit 3 Movies

A *Choose a good title for the passage.*

The Popularity of Hollywood

Surprising Figures for Bollywood Movies

Bollywood vs. Hollywood

Why Bollywood is More Popular than Hollywood

B *Pair up with a partner and ask at least three questions about the passage to each other.*

Q1. _____

Q2. _____

Q3. _____

GLOBAL ACTIVATOR

A *Move around and find someone who has done the following activities. Write their name if they say 'Yes.'*

1. Have you ever seen a Bollywood movie?

2. Do you think Ueto Aya is a great actress?

3. Do you go to movies by yourself?

4. Do you think going to movies is a waste of time?

5. Have you ever held your boy/girlfriend's hand while watching a movie?

6. Would you like to take me to a movie this weekend?

7. *(Your own question)* _____ ?

B *(Optional) Do you agree or disagree with the statements below? Discuss in a pair or small group. Report back to the class.*

- Watching videos at home is better than going to the movies.
- Going on a date at a movie theater is a waste of money. Go somewhere else.
- It's OK to use Indian English as a model for English education in Japan.

19

Unit 4

Dating

Functions

Describing Someone

World Englishes

Mexico

TOPIC QUESTIONS

A *Fill in the blanks with your own information and practice saying them with a partner. Try to be original and informative.*

1. **A:** When did you have your first crush/love?
   B: Well, it was when I was _____.

2. **A:** What was he/she like?
   B: Well, he/she was _____, _____, and very _____.
   (smart / good-looking / cute / honest / attractive / interesting)

3. **A:** What did he/she look like?
   B: He/She had _____ eyes, _____ nose, and _____ hair.
   (big / small / round / straight / curly)

4. **A:** Was he/she tall or short?
   B: Well, he/she was _____ and _____.
   (tall / short / average height / skinny / chubby)

5. **A:** Can you tell me about his/her personality?
   B: Well, he/she was _____, _____, and very _____.
   (funny / easy-going / reliable / friendly / talkative / outgoing)

6. **A:** Which kind of person would you prefer to marry, an attractive but short-tempered person or a not-so-good-looking but very honest and _____ person?
   B: I would prefer a(n) _____ and _____ person because _____.
   (attractive / pretty / good-looking / kind / honest / serious / funny)

B *Change roles and ask the same questions. Be sure to ask and answer follow-up questions.*

Unit 4 Dating

DIALOGUE 🎧 DL 026 💿 CD1-26 ● 🇲🇽 🎧 DL 027 💿 CD1-27 🇺🇸

A *Listen to the conversation and practice with a partner.*

Wataru is talking to his Mexican friend, Maria, before class starts.

Wataru: Was that your <u>boyfriend</u>—the <u>guy</u> walking with you this morning?
Maria: You saw us? Yes, he is.
Wataru: He looks like a nice guy. Tell me about him?
Maria: Well, his name is <u>Jun</u>. He is very <u>tall</u> and <u>good-looking</u>.
Wataru: Yeah. I could tell. He's a <u>good-looking</u> guy.
Maria: Right. But he is rather <u>quiet</u> and kind of <u>shy</u>. And he likes to wear <u>black</u> all the time.
Wataru: Really? Interesting. How did you meet him?
Maria: Well, I met him in the <u>kendo</u> club.
Wataru: You <u>do kendo</u>?
Maria: Yeah, there are many <u>tall</u>, <u>good-looking</u> guys there.
Wataru: What?

B *Replace the underlined words with your own information. Be sure to listen to your partner and change the underlined parts appropriately.*

🎧 DL 028 💿 CD1-28 ● 🇲🇽 🎧 DL 029 💿 CD1-29 🇺🇸

C *Listen to the rest of the conversation and circle T for true, F for false, or U for unknown.*

1. Maria joined the kendo club to meet a tall good-looking man.   **T / F / U**

2. Jun forgot about his date with Maria.   **T / F / U**

3. Maria was waiting for her boyfriend for two hours.   **T / F / U**

4. Maria wasn't very angry about what happened.   **T / F / U**

5. Maria is going to break up with her boyfriend.   **T / F / U**

EXPRESSIONS FOR INTERACTION

A *Practice each dialogue with a partner. Replace the underlined words with your own information.*

Describing Someone's Appearance

1. *A:* **What** is your girlfriend **like**?
   B: She is pretty and very well-dressed.

2. *A:* **Can you describe** George?
   B: Yes, he is of medium-build and wears glasses.

Describing Someone's Personality/Actions

1. *A:* **Mari is very** cute, but a bit short-tempered.
   B: Is that why you broke up with her?

2. *A:* **My boyfriend loves** to meet people and talk.
   B: So he is sociable and talkative.

B *Group the words below into three categories with a partner.*

| stingy | chubby | honest | generous | stupid | attractive | reliable |
| smart | rude | boring | curly hair | skinny | forgetful | friendly | emotional |

appearance

positive personality

negative personality

C *Describe one of the students in your classroom. Your partner needs to find out who you are describing. Take turns. Use the example below to help you.*

Partner: So tell me about someone you have in mind in this class. What is he/she like?

You: Yes, he/she is _____ and _____.

Partner: I see. How about his/her face? What does he/she look like?

You: He/She has a _____ face.

Partner: Can you tell me about his/her hair?

You: Well he/she has _____ hair and it's _____.

Partner: OK. What is he/she wearing?

You: He/She is wearing _____ and _____.

Partner: Does he/she wear glasses?

You: Yes, he/she does. / No, he/she doesn't.

Partner: What is his/her personality like? Is he/she _____?

You: No, he/she is rather _____ and a bit _____.

Partner: I think you're talking about Naoki.

You: Bingo!!

WORLD ENGLISHES

You do NOT need to speak like a native speaker

Can you speak English exactly like a native speaker of English? The answer is NO! No matter how hard you try, you may NOT sound like a native speaker of English because you're NOT. All you have to do is to speak English as an intelligent non-native speaker of English.

The words or sentences below have very difficult sounds for native speakers of Japanese. Try to read them aloud so that people around the world can understand you—even with some Japanese accent. Ask your teacher if your English is good enough as a non-native speaker.

1. narrow, beverages, vehicles, vanilla ice cream, lawn mower, Southern California
2. I don't dare to go there, but Beverly drove to Athens in her old Volvo, not her Mercedes.
3. I regularly play the flute and violin and love to read American literature.

LISTENING ACTIVITIES

Listen to the interview. Take notes and answer the questions.

Notes

Questions

1. What brought her to Japan?
2. How large is her family?
3. What is her favorite Mexican food? What is it like?
4. What is she proud of about Mexico or Mexicans?
5. What is a problem that Mexico has now?

READING ACTIVITIES

Read the passage about Mexico and a problem they face now and fill in the blanks to complete the summary on the next page.

The formal name of Mexico is the United Mexican States. About 60% of the people are Mestizo, people of mixed European and indigenous ancestry, approximately 15% are indigenous, and the rest are mostly of European ancestry. It is the largest Spanish speaking country—113 million people—with a very rich history (32 world heritage sites). It is also the 10th most visited country in the world. But it has one serious problem—obesity.

According to a report by the United Nations 32.8% of Mexicans are obese, the worst in the world followed by Americans at 31.8%. It also reports that almost 70% of Mexicans are overweight. In 1989 the rate was less than 10%. Why the big change? It seems that Mexico quickly became an economic power, and the general public started to consume processed food rather than the traditional vegetables, fruits, and home cooked dishes. Also, many people love soft drinks—the average Mexican drinks 163 liters (46 gallons) of soda each year. That's 40% more than the average American (118 liters, or 31 gallons) and 7.4 times more than the Japanese, who consume on average 22 liters a year. The government is trying to solve the problem by raising taxes for soft drinks. Do you think that will work?

Unit 4 Dating

Summary

The real name of Mexico is (   ) and more than half the number of people in Mexico belong to a (   )-race of people called Mestizo. They speak (   ). People around the world love to (   ) Mexico. The (   ) problem they seem to have is obesity. Over (   )% of the people are overweight and (   )% are very, very fat. The reason for this is the consumption of processed foods and (   ) drinks, which they drink 7.4 times more than Japanese.

GLOBAL ACTIVATOR

A *Write down the name of one famous singer you know well below. Your partner needs to find out who he/she is by asking only YES/NO questions. You can only answer Yes/No. Look at the example.*

Your favorite singer's name: _____

Example

Your partner should ask: **You answer:**
- Is the person female?   Yes.
- Does she sing well?   Yes.
- Is she from Tokyo?   Yes.
- Is she a singer-song-writer?   No.
- Is she a fashion model, too?   Yes.
- Does she wear very unique clothes? Yes.
- Does she have a very long name?   Yes.
- She must be Kyary Pamyu Pamyu!   Yes, you're RIGHT. She is Kyary Pamyu Pamyu.

B *(Optional) What is your image of your ideal future husband/wife like? Tell each other what physical features, personality, possessions, and annual salary he/she has? Give your reasons. Start with "Can you tell me about your future husband/wife?"*

C *(Optional) Which Japanese female singers do you think are going to be more successful in the future? Discuss in a small group. Consider their creativity, physical attractiveness, singing talent, personality, and internationality: Kyary Pamyu Pamyu, Nishino Kana, Amuro Namie, aiko, Ayaka, Utada Hikaru, and Wada Akiko.*

Unit 5

International Food

Functions

Requesting/Restaurant Conversations

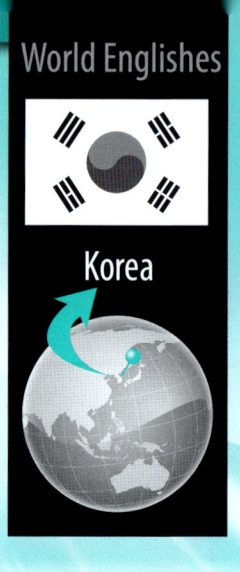

World Englishes

Korea

🌐 TOPIC QUESTIONS

A *Fill in the blanks with your own information and practice saying them with a partner. Try to be original and informative.*

1. *A:* What kinds of food do you like?
   B: I like Chinese, Korean, and _____ food.

2. *A:* What are your favorite dishes?
   B: I like shabu-shabu and _____.

3. *A:* What are your favorite alcoholic drinks?
   B: I like _____ and _____.
   (sake / beer / cocktails / vodka / *shochu*)

4. *A:* What do you cook best?
   B: I can cook _____ pretty well.

5. *A:* What is the strangest food you have ever had?
   B: Well, I've eaten _____ once. (frog legs / raw horse meat)
   It was _____. (very strange / not bad actually)

6. *A:* Would you like to go to a barbecue with me this weekend?
   B: _____. (I'm sorry, I already have plans / Of course)

B *Change roles and ask the same questions. Be sure to ask and answer follow-up questions.*

Unit 5 International Food

DIALOGUE 🎧 DL 033 CD1-33 🇰🇷   🎧 DL 034 CD1-34 🇺🇸

A *Listen to the conversation and practice with a partner.*

Risako traveled to Korea and went into a restaurant on her first day there. She is about to order food in English.

Waitress: 주문 뭐로 하시겠어요?
Risako: Sorry, I don't speak Korean.
Waitress: Oh, English! OK, may I take your order now?
Risako: Yes, I think so. Could I get some *kimchi*?
Waitress: Of course, but *kimchi* comes with every dish. You don't have to order it.
Risako: Really? That's really nice. Then, I'll have *galbi* please?
Waitress: One *galbi*. OK. Anything else?
Risako: Just something to drink. Do you have Pepsi?
Waitress: Sorry, we only have tea and fruit juice.
Risako: Tea is fine, then. Can you make it really hot?
Waitress: Sure. I'll be right back with your *galbi* and hot tea.
Risako: … and *kimchi*.
Waitress: Of course.

B *Replace the underlined words with your own information. Be sure to listen to your partner and change the underlined parts appropriately.*

🎧 DL 035 CD1-35 🇰🇷   🎧 DL 036 CD1-36 🇺🇸

C *Listen to the rest of the conversation and answer the questions.*

1. What does *galbi* come with?

2. What's in the *samgyetang* soup?

3. Is Risako going to have a bowl of rice?

4. What kinds of meat is Risako going to have? Name two.

5. What does Risako order last?

27

EXPRESSIONS FOR INTERACTION

DL 037 CD1-37

A *Practice each dialogue with a partner. Replace the underlined words with your own information.*

Requesting

1. *A:* **Can I get** a <u>Big Mac meal</u>?
   B: Sure. What would you like to drink?

2. *A:* **Do you mind** sitt**ing** <u>at the counter</u>?
   B: If possible, we'd like <u>a table by the window</u>.

Restaurant Language

1. *A:* **May I** take your order now?
   B: Yes, **I'll have** <u>the seafood platter</u>.

2. *A:* **How would you like** your <u>eggs</u>?
   B: (<u>Sunny-side up / Scrambled / Hard boiled / Over easy</u>), **please**.

3. *A:* **Could I interest you in** some dessert?
   B: **No, thank you, but I'd like** <u>a refill on my coffee</u>.

B *Find the best response. Draw a line. Practice with a partner.*

1. How many in your party?-
2. Keep the change.-
3. For here or to go?-
4. What do you have?-
5. Are you ready to order? -
6. Is everything OK?-
7. This is on me.-
8. What is *chawan-mushi*?-
9. What are your specials of the day?-
10. How would you like your steak?-

- We have all kinds of soft drinks.
- No, no. Let's split the bill.
- Thank you, sir.
- Yes, thank you. This is very good.
- No, could you please give us a few more minutes?
- It's a kind of Japanese egg custard.
- Just two of us.
- Today we are serving either fried shrimp or a sashimi combo.
- Medium-rare, please.
- To go, please.

C *Order your lunch, but make it special by making a special request. Follow the example on the next page. Each person must speak twice.*

> **Example** **fried rice and *namul*** (You don't like meat.)
>
> A: I'll have the **fried rice and *namul*?**
>
> B: OK, fried rice and *namul*.
>
> A: Wait. **Can you make the fried rice without meat? I don't like meat.**
>
> B: No problem. No meat.

1. miso ramen and pot stickers   (You like hot and spicy food.)
2. tuna and squid sushi   (You do not like wasabi.)
3. beef curry and coffee   (You like hot curry and weak coffee.)
4. hamburger and cola   (You hate pickles and ice.)
5. soup and salad   (You don't like green peppers and you want non-oil dressing.)

WORLD ENGLISHES

You mean … ?

Sometimes it's difficult to understand English when you hear an unfamiliar accent. If you have a problem understanding what somebody is saying, do not hesitate to ask for repetition or clarification.

Check your understanding by using such phrases as "You mean … ?" "Can you say that again?" "What does … mean?" or "Are you saying … ?" Use the expressions in the parenthesis. Practice with your partner.

> **Example**
>
> A: Sorry there are no trains here.
>
> B: *(take a taxi)* You mean we should take a taxi?

1. A: Drumsticks are everybody's favorite at KFC.
   B: *(chicken legs)* _____
2. A: Your name （name =「ナイム」と発音）, please?
   B: *(my name)* _____
3. A: Use a number two pencil for the test.
   B: *(HB)* _____

LISTENING ACTIVITIES

DL 038　CD1-38

Listen to the interview. Take notes and answer the questions.

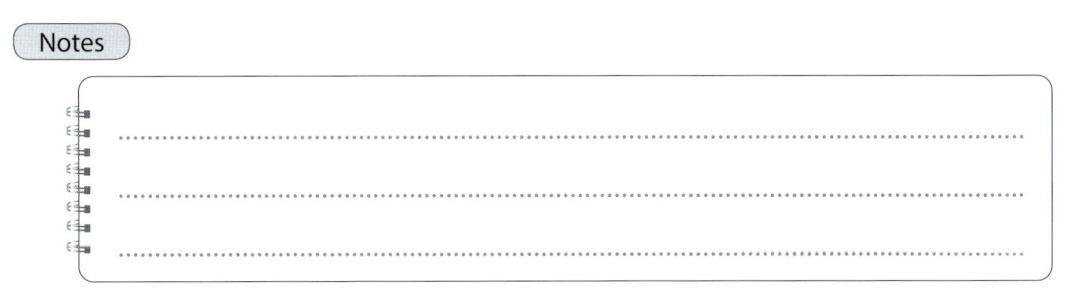

Notes

....
....
....

Questions

1. What does she do in the U.S.?
2. How does she like teaching Japanese in the U.S.?
3. What brought her to the U.S.?
4. Where and how did she learn Japanese?
5. What Korean food does she highly recommend? Why?

READING ACTIVITIES

DL 039　CD1-39

Read the descriptions of some international dishes below. Choose the name of the dishes provided below. You can do this in pairs.

| bibimbap | pho | fish and chips | taco | hamburger |

1. (　　　　　　　　) is a Vietnamese rice noodle soup that has some herbs and meat in it. It is a popular street food in Vietnam and the specialty of a number of restaurant chains around the world. It is primarily served with either beef or chicken.
2. A (　　　　　　　　) is a sandwich consisting of a cooked ground beef patty that is usually placed inside a sliced bun. It is often served with lettuce, bacon, tomato, onion, pickles, cheese and condiments such as mustard, mayonnaise, and ketchup.
3. A (　　　　　　　　) is a traditional Mexican food served in a shell made from cornmeal. It can be made with a variety of fillings, including beef, pork, chicken, vegetables, and cheese, allowing for great versatility and variety.
4. (　　　　　　　　) is an English hot dish, consisting of battered cod and deep-fried potato wedges. People often splash malt vinegar on both parts of this dish. It is a common take-away food.

Unit 5 International Food

5. (_____) is topped with seasoned vegetables such as spinach, mushrooms, carrots, bean sprouts, and served with red pepper paste. Variations often include beef and/or egg. Sometimes it is served in a heated stone bowl.

GLOBAL ACTIVATOR

A *Make a menu for the Global Activator Restaurant. You have to have at least two entries for each category. Exchange books with a partner and order your lunch.*

A: Are you ready to order?
B: Yes, I'll have the _____ lunch.
A: OK, how would you like your eggs?
B: _____, please.
A: You have a choice of sausage or _____.
B: I'll have _____.
A: OK, what kind of salad would you like?
B: _____.
A: What kind of dressing would you like?
B: What do you have?
A: We have _____ and _____.
B: I'll have _____.
A: Would you like anything to drink?
B: I'll have _____.
A: OK, I'll be right back with your _____.

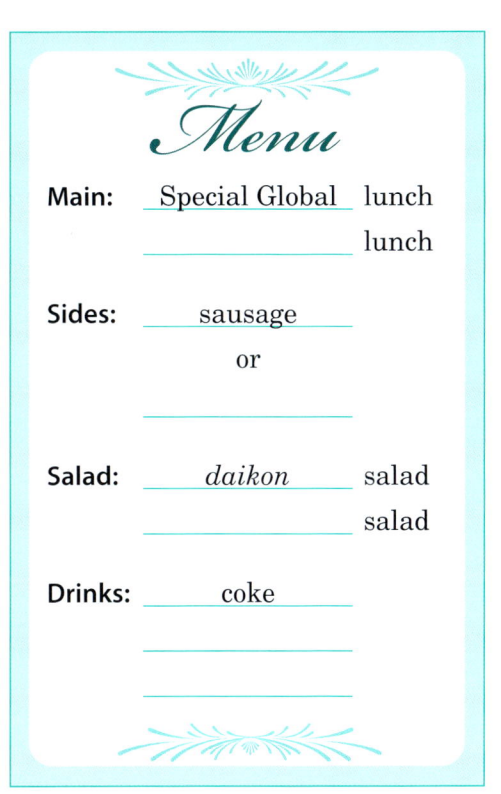

Menu

Main: Special Global lunch
_____ lunch

Sides: sausage
or
_____

Salad: *daikon* salad
_____ salad

Drinks: coke
_____
_____

B *(Optional) In a group of three or four, tell one another the best and the worst food you have ever had. Try to convince the others that your best or worst food is really the best or worst. Give reasons.*

Unit 6

World Englishes

World Englishes

Singapore

Functions

Asking for Repetition/Clarification

TOPIC QUESTIONS

A *Fill in the blanks with your own information and practice saying them with a partner. Try to be original and informative.*

1. *A:* How do you like learning English?
   B: _____. (I love it / Not so much / I hate it)

2. *A:* How did you learn English in elementary school?
   B: By _____ and _____ a lot.
   (singing / dancing / having fun / repeating after the teacher)

3. *A:* How long have you been studying English?
   B: I've been studying for about _____ years.

4. *A:* What kind of English do you speak?
   B: I speak _____ (American / British) English with _____
   (no / some / a thick) Japanese accent.

5. *A:* Do you speak any foreign language other than English?
   B: Yes, I speak _____ a bit. / No, I don't.

6. *A:* Do you know how many official languages Singapore has?
   B: I have no idea. Maybe _____? (two / three / four / five)

B *Change roles and ask the same questions. Be sure to ask and answer follow-up questions.*

Unit 6 World Englishes

DIALOGUE

DL 040　CD1-40　●　🇸🇬　　DL 041　CD1-41　🇺🇸

A *Listen to the conversation and practice with a partner.*

Kenichi is talking to Sophia, a Chinese student from Singapore.

Kenichi: Why are you called <u>Sophia</u>?
Sophia: What? What do you mean?
Kenichi: I mean you're <u>Chinese</u> but you have an English name.
Sophia: In <u>Singapore</u> we all get an English name from <u>our English teacher</u>.
Kenichi: Really? Do you like it?
Sophia: Yeah. I prefer my English name to my <u>Chinese</u> name.
Kenichi: Really? What is your <u>Chinese</u> name?
Sophia: It's <u>Hu Pinni</u>.
Kenichi: Pardon me? Can you say that again?
Sophia: It's <u>Hu, H-U, Pinni, P-I-N-N-I</u>.
Kenichi: What does that mean?
Sophia: It means I'm "<u>kind and friendly</u>."

B *Replace the underlined words with your own/imaginary information. Be sure to listen to your partner and change the underlined parts appropriately.*

DL 042　CD1-42　●　🇸🇬　　DL 043　CD1-43　🇺🇸

C *Listen to the rest of the conversation and circle T for true, F for false, or U for unknown.*

1. Kenichi is the oldest son in his family.　　　　　　　　　T / F / U

2. Singapore has three official languages.　　　　　　　　 T / F / U

3. Sophia spoke English at home when she was very little.　T / F / U

4. The main language of instruction in Singapore is English.　T / F / U

5. Kenichi and Sophia agree that Japanese college students should study English more seriously.　　　　　　　 T / F / U

33

EXPRESSIONS FOR INTERACTION DL 044 CD1-44

A *Practice each dialogue with a partner. Replace the underlined words with your own information.*

Asking for Repetition

1. A: **I'm sorry, could you say that again?**
   B: **I said** <u>you have to use English all the time</u>.

2. A: **I beg your pardon?**
   B: **I said** <u>"Singlish"—it's a unique form of English spoken in Singapore</u>.

Asking for Clarification

1. A: **What do you mean by** that?
   B: Well, **it means** you <u>have to study English seriously</u>.

2. A: Some speak <u>Malay or Tamil</u>.
   B: Some speak **what**?

B *Fill in the blanks. Practice with a partner. A should add one extra sentence.*

1. A: I met someone called Kwok Ting Ting.
   B: You met (   )?

2. A: You need to use Singlish here.
   B: Sorry, I need to use (   ) here?

3. A: (   ) me, but can you say that again?
   B: Sure, I (   ) we should go on a night safari tour.

4. A: What do you mean (   ) being trilingual.
   B: It means they speak three languages.

5. A: Are you (ing) that you can't chew gum in Singapore?
   B: Yes. You may get arrested for chewing gum in Singapore.

6. A: (   ) do you spell Marina Bay Sands?
   B: It's spelled M-A-R-I-N-A B-A-Y (   ).

34

C *Role-play the dialogues from* **B** *again, but this time add one or two more phrases or sentences to continue the dialogue like the example below. Be creative.*

Example

> A: I met someone called Kwok Ting Ting.
> B: You met who?
> A: I said I met someone called Kwok Ting Ting.
> B: What? Is he or she Japanese?
> A: What are you talking about? That sounds nothing like a Japanese name!
> B: Sorry.

WORLD ENGLISHES

International English, please.

English used for international communication should not be too "culture specific."

Ask a partner to use different phrases for what she/he just said. Add "International English, please." or "Could you say that again in plain English?"

1. A: That's really off the wall.
   B: _____.
   A: Sorry, it means it's really stupid or unusual.

2. A: That's like a catch-22.
   B: _____.
   A: Sorry, it means it's impossible or there is no way out.

3. A: Pull the car over.
   B: _____.
   A: Sorry, please stop the car on the side of the road.

LISTENING ACTIVITIES

DL 045　CD1-45

Listen to the interview. Take notes and answer the questions.

Notes

Questions

1. What is her first language?
2. How many languages does she speak?
3. How did she learn her second or third language?
4. What's her advice for Japanese students on learning English?
5. What does she suggest tourists do or see in Singapore?

READING ACTIVITIES

DL 046　CD1-46

Read the passage about "Singlish" and guess the meanings of unique Singlish words to fill in the blanks.

　　Some countries where English is used as a daily communication tool have developed their own variety of English. "Singlish" is one of them. As you can tell, it is a casual form of English developed in Singapore. The Singaporean government, however, heavily discourages the use of Singlish and it has even created an annual "Speak Good English Movement." However, ordinary people still use it every day and many international tourists actually like it because it is very unique and culturally a "rich language."

　　How unique? Well, in Singlish, people often add the word "lah" at the end of each sentence like "Thank you, lah" or "No, lah." Lah does not mean much, but it often softens what you say. They also repeat the same word to emphasize the meaning. For example, if you ask "Can you speak Chinese?" they will answer "Can, can," meaning "Yes, I can." If they say "You *ting ting ting* hard, maybe *den* you get answer," it means "Think hard, then you might understand." Grammar is sometimes simplified. "Can you give me a discount?" often becomes "Discount can, or not?" The answer to this question would be "Yah, can, can." Singlish is very interesting and often user-friendly for Japanese, lah?

Unit 6 World Englishes

1. Dowan. → I don't _____ it. No, thanks.
2. The house sell already. → The house has been _____.
3. Today, pineapples are already gone. Tomorrow can. →
   You _____ tomorrow.
4. You seeing Singapore? → Have you _____ much in Singapore?
5. You're from Japan, is it? → You're from Japan, _____?

GLOBAL ACTIVATOR

A *Try to read each sentence below as fast as you can. Your partner needs to stop you and ask you to slow down and repeat. Use the phrases below. Do not use the same phrase twice.*

- 47% of the Chinese in Singapore speak Mandarin at home.
- Malay is used in the national anthem of Singapore.
- If you forget to flush a toilet in Singapore, you may have to pay a fine of 15,000 yen.
- All traffic signs in Singapore are written in English.
- English seems to be the country's lingua franca despite the fact that four languages are officially used.

You're speaking a little too fast.	Wait. Can you please slow down a bit?
Sorry, I'm not following you.	Excuse me, but could you say that again?
Sorry, I have to do what?	They speak what?

B *(Optional) In a group of three or four, ask each other why your English is not as good as it should be. What went wrong? Discuss in your group.*

■ Was it the way you were taught, the textbooks you used, or your own laziness?
■ Could it be that you just did not have the opportunity to practice your English enough with English speakers around the world?

Unit 7

Weekends/Vacations

Functions

Talking about Free Time

World Englishes

Hong Kong

TOPIC QUESTIONS

A *Fill in the blanks with your own information and practice saying them with a partner. Try to be original and informative.*

1. A: What do you usually do after school?
   B: I usually _____. (go home / go to work / hang out with my friends)

2. A: How was your weekend?
   B: _____. (Just super / Pretty good / Not so good)

3. A: What did you do last weekend?
   B: I _____. (didn't do anything special / went out to *place name*)

4. A: Do you have any plans for next weekend?
   B: Yes, I'm going to / I have to _____. (relax / work)

5. A: What would you like to do this summer?
   B: Well, I'd like to _____.

6. A: Would you like to go with us to Hong Kong this summer?
   B: Hong Kong? Um, _____.
      (of course / let me think about it / I don't think so)

B *Change roles and ask the same questions. Be sure to ask and answer follow-up questions.*

Unit 7 Weekends/Vacations

DIALOGUE

DL 047 CD1-47   DL 048 CD1-48

A *Listen to the conversation and practice with a partner.*

Yuki meets Nancy at the school cafeteria on Monday morning.

Yuki: <u>Nancy</u>! Hi.
Nancy: Hi. <u>Yuki</u>. How was your weekend?
Yuki: Excellent. I had a great time with <u>Mei</u>.
Nancy: Yeah?
Yuki: Yeah. We went out to <u>USJ</u>.
Nancy: Really? That's great! Did you <u>ride the Spiderman ride</u>?
Yuki: I sure did. It was <u>awesome</u>.
Nancy: Yeah? How about <u>that Harry Potter area</u>?
Yuki: We went there, too. It was <u>so scary</u>, but it was <u>so much fun</u>.
Nancy: Good.
Yuki: Yeah, I really had a <u>great</u> time there.
Nancy: I'm so jealous that you <u>got to go there</u>!

B *Replace the underlined words with your own information. Be sure to listen to your partner and change the underlined parts appropriately.*

DL 049 CD1-49   DL 050 CD1-50

C *Listen to the rest of the conversation and answer the questions.*

1. What was the weather like in the afternoon?

2. Did Yuki bring an umbrella?

3. What did Yuki buy to make Mei happy?

4. How was Nancy's weekend?

5. What did Nancy do on Sunday?

39

EXPRESSIONS FOR INTERACTION   DL 051   CD1-51

A *Practice each dialogue with a partner. Replace the underlined words with your own information.*

Talking about Free Time

1. A: **How was your** <u>weekend</u>?
   B: <u>Not bad</u>. Actually, it was **pretty good**.

2. A: **What did you do** <u>over the weekend</u>?
   B: **I didn't do anything special.**

3. A: **What do you usually do** <u>after school</u>?
   B: **I work at** <u>a convenience store</u> <u>every other day</u>.

4. A: **What's your plan for** <u>the summer</u>?
   B: **I'm thinking of** going to <u>Hong Kong</u>.

B *Make questions using the phrases below. Practice with a partner.*

- How was … ?
- Do you have any plans for … ?
- Would you like to … ?
- What's your plan for … ?
- Did you … ?
- What are you ~ing?

1. A: _____ weekend?
   B: Terrible. I lost my wallet and my car broke down.
2. A: _____ Friday evening?
   B: I'm thinking about going to a movie.
3. A: _____ this Saturday?
   B: We're going to the beach.
4. A: _____ this summer?
   B: I'd like to visit my friend in Hong Kong.
5. A: _____ this winter?
   B: Hey, that's great! Let's definitely do that.

C *Imagine your partner is taking a vacation this summer. Ask him/her what they are going to do there.*

Example **Hong Kong**

A: So, you're going to **Hong Kong** this summer. What are you going to do there?

40

B: Well, I'd like to meet Tommy, an old friend of mine.
A: Oh, you have a friend in Hong Kong?
B: Yeah, I met him when he came to our university as an exchange student last year.
A: Good. Are you going to do any sightseeing?
B: Of course. I'm going to climb Victoria Peak and visit Hong Kong Disneyland.
A: Wow. I wish I could join you.

1. Tokyo
2. Hokkaido
3. Disney World in Florida
4. (Your own choice)

WORLD ENGLISHES

Speak loudly

If you're not confident in your English, you may tend to speak quietly, but that will make your English even more difficult for people to understand. If you speak loudly, people will understand you better even if your English has a Japanese accent.

Stand up and face a partner. Stand about FIVE meters apart. Imagine there is a small stream between you and your partner. Now, ask the questions below and two more of your own. You really have to shout! Take turns.

1. Are you having a good time in this class?
2. What are you doing this Friday evening? Do you want to go out for a drink?
3. What's the best tourist spot you've ever been to? Why did you like it so much?
4. (Your own question) _____?
5. (Your own question) _____?

LISTENING ACTIVITIES

DL 052　CD1-52

Listen to the interview. Take notes and answer the questions.

Notes

Questions

1. What brought her to Japan?
2. How did she usually spend her weekends while she was in Hong Kong?
3. How does she usually spend her weekends here in Japan?
4. What do tourists in Hong Kong do?
5. Where does she recommend tourists go in Hong Kong?

READING ACTIVITIES

DL 053　CD1-53

Read the passage about paid vacation around the world.

How often does your father or mother take paid vacation? Statistics show that Japanese workers on average take only five paid vacation days a year, only 38% of the 13 days they could take, the worst of any industrialized nation. Workers in other countries take many more; for example, France 100%, Hong Kong 100%, the U.S. 83% and Korea 70%. That is, 37 days, 12 days, 16 days, and 10 days respectively.

Do Japanese like working so much or are they just too busy? The survey shows that they feel they cannot afford to take vacation and that they fear that their colleagues do not like their coworkers taking vacation, which is a very unique reason for not taking paid vacation. In Germany, there is a law called the "Holiday Law." Under this law every worker has to take about four weeks of vacation a year. Two of these weeks must be consecutive. What a big difference! Maybe Japan should make a similar law.

A *Pair up and ask the questions below.*

1. On average how many paid vacation days do Japanese workers have?
2. On average how many paid vacation days do Japanese workers take?
3. Who seems to take the most number of paid vacation days?
4. What is the unique reason that Japanese people do not take paid vacation days?
5. What is the "Holiday Law" in Germany?

Unit 7 Weekends/Vacations

👥 GLOBAL ACTIVATOR

A *Plan your dream vacation with a partner. Start with the dialogue below.*

A: So, how long do we need for this vacation?
B: _____ (days / weeks / months).
A: Where do you want to go?
B: _____.
A: Why do you want to go there? How about _____?
B: That's fine with me.
A: OK, what do you want to do there?
B: Well, I'd like to _____.
A: What else can we do?
B: We can _____.
A: Should we stay there or move on to another place?
B: _____.
A: *(Your own question)* _____?
B: _____.
A: *(Your own question)* _____?
B: _____.
A: Great! This is going to be fun.
B: Yeah. I can't wait!

B *(Optional) In a group of three or four, ask each other which kind of vacation you would like to take. Discuss it in your group. Give reasons.*

- Do you want to stay home or go to a beach and relax while drinking cocktails? Or do you like to move around while on vacation and do a lot of sightseeing?

C *(Optional) Do you think Japanese work too much? Discuss the questions below in a group. Give reasons.*

- Do you think they should go home earlier and spend more time with their families?
- Do you think it's possible to change this?
- Would you go home right after 5:00?

43

Unit 8

Music/Songs

Functions

Expressing Likes/Dislikes

World Englishes

USA 1
African-American English

TOPIC QUESTIONS

A *Fill in the blanks with your own information and practice saying them with a partner. Try to be original and informative.*

1. *A:* What kind of music do you like?
   B: I like _____. (pop / rock / hip hop / easy listening)

2. *A:* Who is your favorite singer or band? Why?
   B: My favorite singer/band is _____ because _____.

3. *A:* What do you think of (*the name of your favorite musician or band*)?
   B: Oh, I (don't) like him (her/them) because _____.

4. *A:* Have you ever been to a concert?
   B: Yeah, I saw _____ at (*place name*).

5. *A:* Do you play any instruments?
   B: Yes, I play _____. / No, I can't play any instruments.

6. *A:* What is your favorite song to sing at karaoke?
   B: I like to sing _____ because it _____.
   (cheers me up / is relaxing / touches my emotions)

B *Change roles and ask the same questions. Be sure to ask and answer follow-up questions.*

Unit 8 Music/Songs

DIALOGUE DL 054 · CD1-54 · DL 055 · CD1-55

A *Listen to the conversation and practice with a partner.*

Demond, an international student from the U.S., and Rika are talking about music.

Rika: Hey <u>Demond</u>, what's up?
Demond: Nothing much. I was just looking for some new music to put in my <u>phone</u>.
Rika: What kind of music do you like?
Demond: I like <u>just about anything</u>. Do you have any suggestions?
Rika: If you like <u>J-Pop</u>, then I would suggest <u>Hitomi Yamaguchi</u>.
Demond: Why do you like <u>her</u>?
Rika: <u>She</u> has a really <u>great voice</u> and <u>her</u> songs are always <u>upbeat</u>.
Demond: <u>Great</u>. I'll definitely check <u>her</u> out.
Rika: If you like <u>her</u>, maybe you can catch a concert of <u>hers</u> while you're here.
Demond: That would be <u>great</u>. I haven't been to a concert in Japan yet.
Rika: I love going to concerts. I like the <u>energy</u> that I get from going.

B *Replace the underlined words with your own information. Be sure to listen to your partner and change the underlined parts appropriately.*

DL 056 · CD1-56 · DL 057 · CD1-57

C *Listen to the rest of the conversation and answer the questions.*

1. What did Rika suggest that Demond do this summer?

2. According to Rika, why do Japanese artists use English in their songs?

3. According to Demond, what foreign language do many Americans speak?

4. Why do so many Americans speak that language?

5. What does Demond think about Latin music?

45

EXPRESSIONS FOR INTERACTION

DL 058 CD1-58

A *Practice each dialogue with a partner. Replace the underlined words with your own information.*

Expressing Likes

1. *A:* **What do you like about** country music?
   B: **I really like** the instruments that are used.

2. *A:* **What do you think of** J-Pop?
   B: **I love it** because the fast tempo makes me feel like dancing.

Expressing Dislikes

1. *A:* **How do you like** heavy metal?
   B: **Not very much because** it's too loud and makes my ears hurt.

2. *A:* **Do you like** *enka*?
   B: **No, I don't because** it makes me feel like I'm old.

B *Express your likes or dislikes using the phrases below and give reasons. Write your own question and ask that as well.*

> I love/hate it (him/her/them) because …
>
> I sure do. / It's (They're) OK. / Not so much.
>
> I think it's (he's/she's/they're) overrated because …
>
> He's (She's/They're) great/not that great but …

1. What do you think about the name of a popular singer or band?

2. What do you think of rap music (rock / reggae / metal / country music / jazz)?

3. Do you like watching *kouhaku* on New Year's Eve?

4. Do you like listening to J-Pop (K-Pop)?

5. *(Your own question)* _____?

Unit 8 Music/Songs

C *Ask a partner about their likes and dislikes. Be sure to ask him/her the reason why they like or dislike something. He/She has to add "How about you?" at the end and you have to respond as well.*

1. Studying English

2. Horror movies

3. Fast food

4. *(Your own question)*

DL 059 ~ 060   CD1-59 ~ CD1-60

WORLD ENGLISHES

After all, they are all English

There are many varieties of English in the world, but do not think too much about the differences. They have many more common features than differences. After all, they are all English.

Listen to the two sets of passages spoken by two different speakers. In your opinion how different or similar are they in the following areas? Circle your answers.

1. vocabulary   the same   similar   slightly different   very different
2. grammar   the same   similar   slightly different   very different
3. pronunciation   the same   similar   slightly different   very different
4. rhythm/intonation   the same   similar   slightly different   very different
5. meaning   the same   similar   slightly different   very different

LISTENING ACTIVITIES

DL 061　CD1-61

Listen to the interview. Take notes and answer the questions.

Notes

....
....
....

Questions

1. Where in the U.S. is this person from?
2. Why is he going to Japan?
3. What kind of music does he like the most?
4. Why is that his favorite kind of music?
5. What is the name of the band he recommends?

READING ACTIVITIES

DL 062　CD1-62

Read the passage about a type of music and answer the questions.

_____ is a genre of music that originated in the Southern United States with African Americans. It is very difficult to define what _____ is because it is constantly changing and there are many kinds of _____ musicians who often play music using their imagination and not reading music. This is known as improvisation. Another characteristic of _____ is the use of syncopation. Syncopation is when the strong beats in the music are made weak and the weak beats are made strong.

　Some common instruments used in _____ music are the piano, clarinet, saxophone, trombone, trumpet, upright bass, and drums. The drums are usually in the form of a drum set. Guitars are also used in _____, but they are not as common as the other instruments mentioned above.

　One of the most famous _____ musicians was named Dizzy Gillespie. He is known for playing a unique trumpet in a unique way. First, the bell of his trumpet was bent upwards at a 45-degree angle. Second, when Dizzy played this trumpet he puffed out his cheeks. As you can probably guess, Dizzy was born in the Southern U.S.

Unit 8 Music/Songs

A What type of music is being described? Use this ONE word to fill in the blanks.

B Pair up with a partner and ask and answer at least three questions about the reading to each other.

Q1. _____

Q2. _____

Q3. _____

GLOBAL ACTIVATOR

A Find a partner. Ask what types of music he/she likes. Number them from 1 through 10: the most favorite kind of music ⇒ 1, the least favorite ⇒ 10.

| J-pop ( ) | reggae ( ) | heavy metal ( ) | rap ( ) | K-pop ( ) |
| jazz ( ) | country ( ) | classical music ( ) | soul ( ) | rock ( ) |

B Complete the chart by asking your partner questions about his/her favorite type of music or singers. When you're done, find a new partner and tell him/her what you found about your previous partner.

	My Partner	Reason
favorite type of music		
favorite singer		
favorite band		
least favorite type of music		
least favorite singer or band		

49

Unit 9

Sports

World Englishes

Australia

Functions

Commenting/Expressing Feelings

TOPIC QUESTIONS

A Fill in the blanks with your own information and practice saying them with a partner. Try to be original and informative.

1. *A:* What sports do you like?
   B: I like _____.

2. *A:* Who is your favorite athlete?
   B: My favorite athlete is _____ because he/she is _____.
   (talented / inspiring / a hard worker)

3. *A:* What is your favorite sports team?
   B: My favorite sports team is _____ because _____.

4. *A:* What team do you hate?
   B: I hate _____ because _____.

5. *A:* What do you think of (*the name of athlete or sports team*) this year?
   B: I think (he/she/they) (is/are) _____.
   (great / awful / OK / not so good)

6. *A:* Do you often go to sporting events?
   B: Well, I go to _____ (watch baseball/sumo / cheer for our school's rugby team) _____. (very often / once a year or so)

B Change roles and ask the same questions. Be sure to ask and answer follow-up questions.

50

Unit 9 Sports

DIALOGUE DL 063 · CD2-02 🇯🇵 🇦🇺   DL 064 · CD2-03 🇺🇸

A *Listen to the conversation and practice with a partner.*

Mark, an international student from Australia, and Aya are talking about sports.

Aya: Have you joined any clubs at the university here?
Mark: No, but I was thinking about <u>rugby</u>.
Aya: You're a <u>big guy</u>. You must <u>be good at rugby</u>.
Mark: <u>I do okay</u>. I've played since <u>high school</u>. Are you in a club?
Aya: Yes, I'm on the <u>lacrosse</u> team.
Mark: I don't know much about <u>lacrosse</u>. How is it played?
Aya: It's kind of like <u>soccer, but with sticks</u>.
Mark: I'd like to watch you play sometime.
Aya: We practice <u>every day from five to six</u>. Feel free to come anytime and watch.
Mark: Thanks! I always get <u>excited</u> when I watch sports.

B *Replace the underlined words with your own information. Be sure to listen to your partner and change the underlined parts appropriately.*

DL 065 · CD2-04 🇯🇵 🇦🇺   DL 066 · CD2-05 🇺🇸

C *Listen to the rest of the conversation and answer the questions.*

1. What does Mark like to watch the most?

2. What sport has Mark watched live in Japan?

3. What sport is popular in Australia?

4. What did Mark watch on TV?

5. Where is Mark living?

6. What is special about Aya's friend?

EXPRESSIONS FOR INTERACTION

A *Practice each dialogue with a partner. Replace the underlined words with your own information.*

Expressing Positive Feelings

1. A: **What does it feel like when** you score a goal?
   B: **It feels** great. **It feels like** you are the best in the world.

2. A: **Why do you like** jogging?
   B: **I like** jogging because I feel that I have more energy when I am done.

Expressing Negative Feelings

1. A: The Dragons **are doing excellent** these days.
   B: **I have to disagree.** They are **terrible**.

2. A: **Are you a good** baseball **player**?
   B: **I'm okay, but I get** frustrated **when I** strike out.

B *Work with a partner. Use the phrases to express positive, negative, and neutral feelings to answer the questions below. Then give reasons as well.*

positive feelings	negative feelings	neutral feelings
• I could die happily if …	• I feel terrible.	• I don't care much about it.
• I love it.	• I hate it.	• It's okay, but it's not for me.
• I feel so excited.	• It's disappointing.	• Not too bad.

1. What do you think of water sports?
2. How do you feel when you lose a game?
3. How do you feel when you win a game?
4. Do you like watching soccer?
5. Which do you like better, watching sports or playing sports?
6. *(Your own question)* _____?

C *Give your comments or how you feel about the following questions. Use the phrases on the next page and make sure you talk with a partner for at least one minute.*

Unit 9 Sports

• How do you like … ?	• Sorry, I don't agree.
• What do you think of … ?	• I feel differently; I feel …
• How about you?	• I know what you mean.

1. Running on a treadmill to lose weight

2. Riding a roller coaster

3. The Japanese national soccer team, *Samurai Blue*

4. *(Your own question)*

WORLD ENGLISHES

Say "I" first, then think

Sometimes you can't think of good words or phrases to express your thoughts and you stay quiet. Be confident. Your English is good enough. Just say "I," then think. Surprisingly, this "I" will pull out the expression or phrases you need.

Keep saying "I" until you think of something to say. Practice with a partner.

1. *You:* What would you do if you had a billion yen?
   Partner: I, I, I, I think I would …
2. *You:* You want to go see the soccer game with me this weekend?
   Partner: I think, I think, I, I …
3. *You:* What foreign country would you like to visit the most?
   Partner: I, I would like to …
4. *You:* How do you like speaking in front of a lot of people?
   Partner: I, I, I …

LISTENING ACTIVITIES

DL 068　CD2-07

Listen to the interview. Take notes and answer the questions.

Notes

....
....
....

Questions

1. Where in Australia is this person from?
2. Why did he come to Japan?
3. What sports does he like to play?
4. How does he feel when he scores?
5. What is the name of his favorite team?

READING ACTIVITIES

DL 069　CD2-08

Read the passage about a unique sport called cricket and answer the questions.

　　Australians love to play sports. It is estimated that about 70% of the nation plays some kind of sport at least once a week and over 44% three times or more a week. In the Olympics they always get many more medals than Japan, although the population of Australia is only one-sixth that of Japan.

　　They enjoy such sports as walking, jogging, swimming, tennis, and golf just like any other nation, but they also play some very unique sports. Among them is cricket. It's a game that uses a bat and ball. Unlike baseball, the team in the field has eleven players. The bowler, similar to the pitcher in baseball, delivers the ball by swinging his arm over his head. The bowler tries to hit the wicket with the ball. The wicket is made up of stumps and bails. The stumps are three sticks that are pushed into the ground. The bails are two smaller sticks that are balanced on top of the stumps. The batsman tries to defend the wicket by hitting the ball. Once he hits the ball, he runs toward the other wicket to score a run. Too complicated? Indeed. You may have to live in Australia, England, or India to fully understand and enjoy this unique sport.

Unit 9 Sports

A *Use the information from the passage to label the pictures.*

B *Pair up with a partner and ask at least three questions about the passage to each other.*

Q1. _____

Q2. _____

Q3. _____

GLOBAL ACTIVATOR

A *Write the names of two teams or athletes that you know well. With a partner talk about them. Be sure you and your partner both express your opinions.*

1. _____   2. _____

Example

A: I don't really like the Giants. They are just a rich team. What do you think?

B: I agree. Most people only like them because the media tells them to like them.

A: Exactly. They are almost like the New York Yankees, but ...

B: ...

B *(Optional) Do you agree or disagree with the statements below? Discuss in a pair or small group. Report back to the class.*

- Soccer is more difficult than baseball.
- Playing sports is really good for children.
- Watching sports on TV is better than watching them at a stadium.

Unit 10

Shopping

Functions

Negotiating/Expressions for Shopping

World Englishes

China

TOPIC QUESTIONS

A Fill in the blanks with your own information and practice saying them with a partner. Try to be original and informative.

1. *A:* Do you like shopping? Why or why not?
   B: I (don't) like shopping because _____.
   (I get what I want / it makes me happy/tired / it reduces my stress)

2. *A:* Where do usually go shopping?
   B: I usually go to _____ to shop.

3. *A:* Do you ask for a discount when you buy something expensive?
   B: Yes / No / It depends, because _____.
   (I'm buying expensive stuff / I'm too shy / it doesn't hurt to try)

4. *A:* Do you like to buy big brand name goods?
   B: Yes, I do / No, I don't. It's because they are _____.
   (elegant / well-made / colorful / pretty / too gaudy / overpriced)

5. *A:* What do you think of (*the name of a brand*)?
   B: I think _____.
   (it's really nice/well-designed/gorgeous/OK / I really don't care)

6. *A:* Do you ever buy second-hand goods?
   B: Yes / No, because _____.

B Change roles and ask the same questions. Be sure to ask and answer follow-up questions.

Unit 10 Shopping

DIALOGUE DL 070 · CD2-09 ● DL 071 · CD2-10

A *Listen to the conversation and practice with a partner.*

Wang Qian, an international student from China, and Ryusei are talking about shopping.

Ryusei: Wang Qian, what are you doing this weekend?
Wang Qian: I don't have anything planned. Is something going on?
Ryusei: There's a new restaurant that is opening and some of my friends and I are going to check it out. Would you like to join us?
Wang Qian: Sure, that'd be great. Where is it?
Ryusei: It's by the mall on Route 19. You can go with us or meet us there.
Wang Qian: I think I'll meet you there because I need to get something at the electronics store.
Ryusei: That's fine. If you can't find us, just give me a call.

B *Replace the underlined words with your own information. Be sure to listen to your partner and change the underlined parts appropriately.*

DL 072 · CD2-11 ● DL 073 · CD2-12

C *Listen to the rest of the conversation and answer the questions.*

1. What does Wang Qian need to buy?

2. Where does Ryusei suggest Wang Qian buy ink?

3. What items does Ryusei say you can negotiate the price on?

4. According to Ryusei, why do Japanese people buy a lot of stuff when they are overseas?

5. Where in Japan does Wang Qian say you can get things for a really cheap price?

57

EXPRESSIONS FOR INTERACTION

DL 074 CD2-13

A *Practice each dialogue with a partner. Replace the underlined words with your own information.*

> **Expressions for Shopping**
>
> 1. *A:* Welcome to <u>Tom's Tank Tops</u>. **Can I help you find <u>something</u>?**
>   *B:* **<u>No, thank you</u>. I'm <u>just browsing</u>.**
>
> 2. *A:* **Do you have this in <u>another size</u>?**
>   *B:* Yes, we do. What <u>size</u> were you looking for?
>
> 3. *A:* **Excuse me, I'm looking for <u>the men's department</u>.**
>   *B:* It's <u>straight back and to the right</u>.
>
> 4. *A:* **Can you give me a discount?**
>   *B:* Let's see. **I can give it to you for <u>2,000 yen</u>.** How's that?

B *The sentences below are scrambled. Unscramble the sentences to find useful phrases for shopping. Practice saying them with a partner, then write them on the line.*

1. *A:* (try / can / on / I / this) _____?
   B: (here / the / room / is / fitting / over) Sure, _____.

2. *A:* (bit / this / a / tight / is / too) _____.
   (this / have / in / bigger / a / size) Do you _____?
   B: (size / are / of / out / that / we) Sorry, _____.

3. *A:* (you / OK / everything / did / find) _____?
   B: Yes, thank you.
   A: (be / cash / charge / that / or) Will _____?
   B: (you / JCB / take) Do_____?

4. *A:* (warranty / for / is / the / this / TV / long)
   How _____?
   B: (you / extend it / year, / but / pay extra / can / if you)
   It's one _____.

Unit 10 Shopping

C *Read the roles below carefully and role-play a sales clerk and customer. Use the pictures or your own idea for the items you want to buy.*

Sales clerk: You try not to give the customer a bargain.
Customer: You try to get a large discount from the sales clerk.

A: May I help you?
B: Yes, I'm looking for _____.
A: They are right over here.
B: Thank you. How much is this _____?
A: It's only _____.
B: Can you give me a discount?
A: No, that's the best we can do.
B: Well, let me try them on first, then.
A: Sure, the fitting room is _____.

(*continue the conversation on your own*)

B: How about _____ yen? I'll pay you cash.
A: No, how about _____ with no tax?
B: Fine. Thank you.
A: Thank YOU for shopping with us.

WORLD ENGLISHES

Is Japanese English so bad?

Some English vocabulary words have Chinese or Japanese origin. For example, the English word "ketchup" is said to come from the Cantonese word for "tomato juice." "Hibachi" is also an English word for a type of grill used to cook meat with charcoal. Maybe we should promote more Japanese phrases that could be the next English words. Can you think of any candidates? Ask your teacher if the words below have some possibilities.

1. *washlet   mottainai   kawaii   yoroshiku*
2. **dead ball   paper driver   gasoline stand   note** *paso-con* **(laptop)**
3. I was so tired that **I slept like mud** yesterday. (I slept like a log.)
4. I think he has **a black belly**. (He is evil-minded.)

LISTENING ACTIVITIES

DL 075 CD2-14

Listen to the interview. Take notes and answer the questions.

Notes

....

....

....

Questions

1. Where in China is this person from?
2. Why did she come to the U.S.?
3. What does she like to shop for?
4. Why are cars and luxury products more expensive in China?
5. What is very expensive in Japan?

READING ACTIVITIES

DL 076 CD2-15

Read the passage about shopping styles in the U.S. and China and answer the questions.

Have you heard of Black Friday or Cyber Monday? They are the days when shops around the U.S. have special sales. Black Friday is the day after Thanksgiving, when the Christmas shopping season starts. Shops offer bargains that consumers can't resist. The real reason it is called Black Friday is not known, but some people say it is because that is when shops start to make a profit, or move from the red to the black. Cyber Monday follows just a few days after Black Friday, when big discounts online can be gotten. The term made its debut on November 28, 2005 and has become very popular in the U.S. and around the world.

China also has a big shopping season, which is right before the Chinese New Year. New Year festivities traditionally last 15 days, so people go shopping for a lot of food, new clothes, and gifts for relatives. Today, some wealthy Chinese people go shopping overseas while on vacation. One report says that Chinese consumers now make two-thirds of their luxury purchases abroad. The report also says there are 600 billionaires in China and 2.8 million millionaires, measured in U.S. dollars. *The China Daily* also reported that Chinese travelers spent $89 billion while overseas in one year. Many brand name boutiques employ Chinese-speaking sales clerks to welcome Chinese shoppers.

Unit 10 Shopping

A *Pair up and ask at least one question to each other about the topics below. Do NOT write anything. Just talk.*

1. About Black Friday (What is … ? / When is … ? / Why is it called … ?)
2. About Cyber-Monday (What is … ? / When is … ? / Why is it called … ?)
3. About the Chinese shopping season (When is … ? / How long … ?)
4. About shopping overseas made by wealthy Chinese (Where … ? / How much … ?)
5. About billionaires or millionaires in China (How many … ? / How much … ?)

B *What do they mean? Explain in English to a partner.*

1. Billionaires are those people who _____.
2. Millionaires are those people who _____.
3. $89 billion is equal to about _____ Japanese yen.

GLOBAL ACTIVATOR

A *Take turns asking the following questions with a partner to find out about each other's shopping experiences. Make sure to take turns asking questions or giving comments to each other.*

1. Do you like to shop? (follow-up question: Why don't/do you like to shop?)
2. How often do you go shopping?
3. Where do you usually go shopping?
4. Do you have something you want to shop for now?
5. Which do you prefer, shopping alone or with your friends?
6. Have you negotiated a lower price on something you've bought?
7. Have you bought something on the Internet?
8. What do you think of a person who always buys big brand name goods?
9. If you had 100,000 yen to spend for a suit, which would you like to get, an expensive nice suit or three inexpensive not-so-nice suits? Why?
10. *(Your own question)* _____?

B *(Optional) Do you agree or disagree with the statements below. Discuss in a pair or small group. Report back to the class.*

- It is never safe to buy something on the Internet.
- It is best to always pay cash when you are shopping.
- Higher prices always means higher quality.

Unit 11

Traveling/Studying Overseas

Functions

Expressions for Traveling

World Englishes

USA 2
Midwestern English

TOPIC QUESTIONS

A Fill in the blanks with your own information and practice saying them with a partner. Try to be original and informative.

1. *A:* Have you ever been overseas?
   B: No, I haven't. / Yes, I've been to _____.

2. *A:* Do you like to travel? Why or why not?
   B: I (don't) like to travel because _____.
   (I like different cultures / it's a way of recharging / I can't afford it)

3. *A:* If you could travel anywhere in the world, where would you like to go?
   B: I'd like to go to _____ because _____.

4. *A:* Would you like to study abroad?
   B: Yes, I'd like to study in _____ because _____.
   No, I wouldn't because _____.
   (I want to make international friends / I'm not interested / I'm scared)

5. *A:* Do you prefer to travel by train, bus, car, or airplane?
   B: I prefer to travel by _____ because _____.

6. *A:* What is the best place you've ever visited?
   B: The best place I've ever visited is _____. It was great because _____.

B Change roles and ask the same questions. Be sure to ask and answer follow-up questions.

Unit 11 Traveling/Studying Overseas

DIALOGUE DL 077 CD2-16   DL 078 CD2-17

A Listen to the conversation and practice with a partner.

Jack, an international student from the U.S., and Maki are talking about travel.

Maki: Hi Jack! How was your trip to Kyoto?
Jack: It was great! The best part was when we went to *Sanjusangen-do*.
Maki: I really like that place, too.
Jack: What did you do over the weekend?
Maki: I was planning some side trips for when I go to the States. Maybe you can help me.
Jack: Sure. Where do you want to go?
Maki: I want to go to Orlando because they have so many theme parks. I'm not sure the best way to get there from Ohio.
Jack: The best way would be to fly there. It costs more than taking a bus, but you'll save a lot of time.
Maki: Thanks.

B Replace the underlined words with your own information. Be sure to listen to your partner and change the underlined parts appropriately.

 DL 079 CD2-18   DL 080 CD2-19

C Listen to the rest of the conversation and circle T for true or F for false.

1. It takes about twenty hours to go to Orlando by bus.   T / F
2. It takes about two and a half hours to fly to Orlando.   T / F
3. Jack uses his computer to check the prices for the bus and airplane.   T / F
4. Maki is going to study at Florida University.   T / F
5. Maki decides to go to Orlando by airplane.   T / F

EXPRESSIONS FOR INTERACTION

DL 081 CD2-20

A *Practice each dialogue with a partner. Replace the underlined words with your own information.*

Expressions to Use while Traveling

1. *A:* **Excuse me, does this bus go to Easton Town Center?**
   B: No, it doesn't. This one goes to Pacific Mall.

2. *A:* **Could you please tell me how to get to Times Square?**
   B: Sure. Just take the C Line to 42nd Street.

3. *A:* **What is a good restaurant to try around here?**
   B: You should definitely go to Skyline Chili.

4. *A:* **Hello, my name is Kenji Kimura. I have a reservation.**
   B: Welcome, Mr. Kimura. We have a reservation for you staying with us for 3 nights.

B *Choose the correct word for each space. Practice saying them with a partner.*

1. *A:* When do you arrive?
   B: We arrive (in / at / for) New York (from / at / on) 6:45 P.M.

2. *A:* How are you getting to the hotel?
   B: We're going to go (in / on / by) taxi.

3. *A:* What are you going to do tomorrow?
   B: We're going to go (to / on / until) the Statue of Liberty.

4. *A:* What are you going to do after that?
   B: We're going to get (to / on / by) the subway and go to Times Square.

5. *A:* How long will you be here?
   B: We'll be here (by / at / until) next Saturday.

Unit 11 Traveling/Studying Overseas

C You and your partner are going to take several trips together. Plan trips to the places below. Use the example to help you.

Example **Canada**

A: So we're going to Canada. What would you like to do first?
B: I think we should go to Niagara Falls.
A: That sounds great. What can we do there?
B: We can take a boat and go to the bottom of the falls.
A: That sounds like fun. I'd like to walk to the U.S. from Canada.
B: Wonderful! We can take a picture of us standing in two countries at the same time!

1. Kyoto
2. London
3. Seoul
4. Rome
5. *(Your own idea)*

WORLD ENGLISHES

"Wasei-eigo"

Some English words made in Japan, "wasei-eigo," are very unique and could be used in international communication as we have shown in Unit 10 (p. 59). However, some "wasei-eigo" words may not make sense at all to non-Japanese. What would be good English words for the following "wasei-eigo?" The first one is done for you.

1. consent ⇒ (outlet)
2. guts pose ⇒ (success / _____ pose)
3. Doctor helicopter ⇒ (_____ ambulance)
4. virgin road ⇒ (the aisle the _____ walks down)
5. cunning ⇒ (_____ on a test)
6. American dog (a type of food) ⇒ (_____)
7. new half ⇒ (_____ / shemale / drag queen)
8. ten keys ⇒ (_____ pad)

LISTENING ACTIVITIES

DL 082　CD2-21

Listen to the interview. Take notes and answer the questions.

Notes

....
....
....

Questions

1. Where in the U.S. is this person from?
2. Why did she come to Japan?
3. What are the best places she's been to in Japan?
4. Where would she like to go to next?
5. What other country would she like to visit? Why?

READING ACTIVITIES

DL 083　CD2-22

Read the descriptions of some famous places to travel. Work with a partner to match the name of the place with its description.

Bahamas　　Montreal　　Yellowstone　　San Francisco　　Jerusalem

1. (　　　　　) If you fell asleep and woke up in this city, you would think you were in France, but you wouldn't be. The people in this city speak French. It might be best to visit sometime between May and October. The winter might be too cold because this city is in Canada.

2. (　　　　　) If you like the outdoors, then you will love this national park located in the U.S. Some great things to see here are geysers (hot water that shoots out from the ground), animals such as bison, bear, and antelope, and hot springs that come in many different colors.

3. (　　　　　) This city is the Holy City for three major religions: Christianity, Judaism, and Islam. It is located in Israel. There are many historical sites that you can visit. The Dead Sea is also located close to this city. It is called the Dead Sea because there is so much salt in it that nothing can live there. If you go in the Dead Sea, you will float!

4. (   ) This city is known for a famous bridge named The Golden Gate Bridge. You can enjoy riding up and down the hills of this city on its famous streetcars. Don't forget to get some Chinese food as this city in the U.S. is also known for its large Chinese community.

5. (   ) Do you like the beach? If so, you'll love this place. It's made up of several islands. As you can imagine, this is a great place to go to the beach, explore the reefs while snorkeling and scuba diving and you can even enjoy shopping in this tropical paradise.

GLOBAL ACTIVATOR

A *Move around and find someone who has done the following activities. If a person answers 'yes' then write that person's name. Be sure to ask follow-up questions. Start with, "Have you … ?" or "Do you … ?"*

Find someone who	Names
1. has been to the U.S.	( )
2. has studied abroad	( )
3. has never flown in an airplane	( )
4. has done a homestay	( )
5. has ridden on a ferry	( )
6. has helped a lost tourist in Japan	( )
7. wants to study abroad	( )
8. wants to travel around the world	( )
9. prefers traveling alone to traveling with someone	( )
10. *(Your own idea)* _____ ?	( )

B *(Optional) Do you agree or disagree with the statements below? Discuss in a pair or small group. Report back to the class with your reasons.*

- More Japanese students should study abroad.
- Asia is a better place to visit than Europe.
- The best time to go on vacation is in the spring or fall when the weather is nice.

Unit 12

Festivals/Parties

World Englishes: Germany

Functions

Asking Favors/Asking for Permission

TOPIC QUESTIONS

A Fill in the blanks with your own information and practice saying them with a partner. Try to be original and informative.

1. A: Do you like to go to parties or festivals?
   B: Yes, I do / No, I don't because _____.
   (they are fun/boring/too crowded / I can meet new people)

2. A: How often do you go to parties?
   B: I go to parties _____.
   (once in a while / sometimes / pretty often / every weekend)

3. A: What kinds of parties do you like?
   B: I really like _____ (drinking / dinner / Christmas / birthday / cookouts) (parties) because _____.

4. A: Why don't Japanese people usually have parties at their homes?
   B: Well, it's because _____.
   (their houses are too small / it's too troublesome / they don't want to show people their homes)

5. A: What is the most famous festival in your area?
   B: The _____ festival. It's a festival celebrating _____.

6. A: We're having a cookout this Saturday. You want to come?
   B: _____. (Of course / Let me think about it / Who else is coming?)

B Change roles and ask the same questions. Be sure to ask and answer follow-up questions.

Unit 12 Festivals/Parties

DIALOGUE

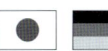

DL 084　CD2-23　　　　DL 085　CD2-24

A *Listen to the conversation and practice with a partner.*

Jana, an international student from Germany, and Takuma are talking about travel.

Jana: Hi Takuma. Do you mind if I join you for lunch?
Takuma: No, not at all. Please sit down. Are you enjoying your time in Japan?
Jana: Yes I am. Everybody is so nice. I went to a party last weekend.
Takuma: What kind of party was it?
Jana: It was a birthday party for my friend's boyfriend.
Takuma: Did you have a good time?
Jana: I sure did. I realized that Japanese people don't have many parties at their homes.
Takuma: That's right. Most homes are too small and people don't want to clean up. It's easier to have parties at a restaurant.
Jana: That makes sense. Anyway, we had a great time.

B *Replace the underlined words with your own information. Be sure to listen to your partner and change the underlined parts appropriately.*

DL 086　CD2-25　　　　DL 087　CD2-26

C *Listen to the rest of the conversation and answer the questions.*

1. What does Jana like about festivals in Japan?

2. When is Takuma going to a festival?

3. What is the festival near?

4. What kind of festival is it?

5. What is Jana going to make at the festival?

6. What alcoholic drink is she a big fan of?

EXPRESSIONS FOR INTERACTION   DL 088   CD2-27

A *Practice each dialogue with a partner. Replace the underlined words with your own information.*

Asking Favors

1. A: **Can you** meet me at <u>the station before the party</u>?
   B: **Sure, no problem.**

2. A: **Will you do me a favor? Could you** <u>work for me tomorrow night</u>?
   B: **I'm sorry. I already have plans for** <u>tomorrow night</u>.

Asking for Permission

1. A: **May I** take a look at <u>your festival schedule</u>?
   B: **Sure,** here you go. / **Sorry,** it's not mine.

2. A: **Do you mind if** <u>I bring my girlfriend to your party</u>?
   B: No, **I'd be glad to** <u>meet her</u>. /
      I'm sorry. It's <u>formal and we only have enough for the people invited</u>.

B *There are different levels of politeness and formality for asking a favor or for permission. Study the chart.*

casual	polite / formal	more polite and formal
for anyone	for bigger requests	for teachers / bosses
Can you … ?	**Could you … ?**	**May I … ?** **Do you mind … ?**

Make the conversations below more polite or formal. Practice with a partner twice.

First time: You're talking to a student who is older than you (your *senpai*).
Second time: You're talking to a teacher who is over 60 years old.

1. A: Can you bring some wine to the party?
   B: Sure, no problem.
2. A: Take me home now, will you? I'm too tired from the party.
   B: OK. Just a second.
3. A: Can you pay 4,000 yen for the party in advance?
   B: Sorry, I can't. I'm broke now.

70

Unit 12 Festivals/Parties

C *Think of the best way to ask a favor or for permission in the situations below. Act out the conversation with a partner. Use "Can/Could you … ?," "Can/Could/May I … ?," or "Do you mind if … ?"*

Example

You have no money for the party tonight. You want to borrow some from your friend.

A: I left my wallet at home today. **Could I** borrow some money for the party?
B: Of course, but I have to get some from the ATM first.
A: Thank you. I really appreciate it.

1. You forgot your homework. You want to ask your teacher if you can submit it late.
2. You don't have an eraser. You want to borrow one from a classmate.
3. You need to go to the restroom during class. How should you ask your teacher for permission?
4. Your friend is leaving the party in her car. You want her to drive you home and you live close to each other.

WORLD ENGLISHES

Rhythm and Intonation > Pronunciation

Rhythm and intonation make a bigger difference than the sounds of each specific word in communication. Do not worry too much about how good your pronunciation is, but do pay attention to whether or not your English has good rhythm and intonation. Make sure your English isn't too CHOPPY.

Try to read the next sentences fast and see if your partner or teacher can understand you?

1. ケナヤブ your pen for a second?
2. ジュワナ come to my birthday party this weekend?
3. ジュマイン・デファイ ask some other friends to come along?
4. ケニュ・テイカワ picture?
5. "レリゴ・レリゴー Can't 堀場ッ anymore …" フーさん this song?
6. Come over here and 知らんぷりー.
7. "メリケン Idol" was created based on the British show "パッパイドッ."

LISTENING ACTIVITIES

DL 089   CD2-28

Listen to the interview. Take notes and answer the questions.

Notes

```
................................................................................................
................................................................................................
................................................................................................
```

Questions

1. Where in Germany is this person from?
2. What is she doing in Japan?
3. What festival has she really enjoyed in Japan?
4. What is the best festival in Germany?
5. Why is that festival the best?

READING ACTIVITIES

DL 090   CD2-29

Read the passage about a famous festival in Germany and fill in the blanks to complete the summary on the next page.

Probably the most famous festival in Germany is Oktoberfest. This festival started in Munich back in 1810. As you can guess, this festival has something to do with the month of October. The festival runs for sixteen or seventeen days starting towards the end of September and ending during the first weekend in October. Most people associate Oktoberfest with drinking beer, but not just any beer can be sold at Oktoberfest.

A beer must be brewed according to what is known as the German Beer Purity Law. Beers that are made according to this "law" must contain certain ingredients. Another condition is that the beer must have been brewed within the city limits of Munich. If those conditions are met, then the beer can be sold at this great festival. Approximately seven million liters of beer are sold at this event each year.

Festivalgoers also have a chance to try some of the food of Germany. Some traditional foods are roast chicken and pork, grilled ham, sausages, pretzels, potato pancakes, and sauerkraut. In addition to food, those attending the event can enjoy various attractions such as rides or games.

Unit 12 Festivals/Parties

Summary

(   ) is a famous festival in (   ) that began in the 19th century. It is usually held in (   ) and October. Many people enjoy drinking (   ) at this festival. The (   ) that is sold at this festival must be (   ) within the city of (   ).
In addition to this fine drink, you can also try some German (   ), such as sausages or pretzels.

GLOBAL ACTIVATOR

A *Move around and find someone who has done the following activities. If a person answers 'yes' then write that person's name. Be sure to ask follow-up questions such as "How was it?," "Are you serious?" and "Tell me more."*

Have you ever … ? / Do you … ?	Names
1. has been to an Oktoberfest or *Aki-matsuri* in Japan	( )
2. has been to a festival in a different prefecture	( )
3. has missed the train because of a party	( )
4. has been to a party with non-Japanese people	( )
5. prefers playing games at home to going to parties	( )
6. drank too much at a party and had a hangover next day	( )
7. does not mind being an organizer of a party, *kanji-san*	( )
8. hasn't been to a party for a long time	( )
9. would like to have a karaoke party with you	( )
10: *(Your own idea)* _____ ?	( )

B *(Optional)* **With your group, design a new festival in your area. Be sure to include the following information.**

- What kind of festival is it?
- What can people do at the festival?
- What is unique about your festival?
- Where will the festival be held?
- How long will the festival be?

Unit 13

Part-time/Future Jobs

Functions

Functions: Conveying Intentions/Future Plans

World Englishes

Brazil

TOPIC QUESTIONS

A Fill in the blanks with your own information and practice saying them with a partner. Try to be original and informative.

1. *A:* Do you have a part-time job?
   B: Yes, I do. / No, I don't because _____.
   (I need to work / I'm too busy with school work)

2. *A:* (If yes) Do you like your job?
   (If not) Do you want to work part-time?
   B: Yes, I do / No, I don't because _____.
   (the pay is good / I enjoy meeting people)

3. *A:* What would you like to do after you graduate?
   B: I'd like to work for/become _____ because I enjoy _____.

4. *A:* What jobs do you think are good jobs?
   B: I think _____ and _____ are good jobs.

5. *A:* Why do you think the jobs you mentioned above are good jobs?
   B: Because _____. (they pay you well / they are challenging)

6. *A:* At what age would you like to get married? How about buying your first house?
   B: I'd like to get married at the age of _____ and have a house built by the time I'm _____.

B Change roles and ask the same questions. Be sure to ask and answer follow-up questions.

Unit 13 Part-time/Future Jobs

DIALOGUE

DL 091　CD2-30　　　　DL 092　CD2-31

A *Listen to the conversation and practice with a partner.*

Mariana, an international student from Brazil, and Kota are talking about jobs.

Mariana: Hi Kota. What's up?
Kota: I'm looking for a part-time job on the net.
Mariana: What kind of job are you looking for?
Kota: I want a job that lets me cook.
Mariana: Why?
Kota: Because I like to cook.
Mariana: I see. Would you rather work in fast food or in a regular restaurant?
Kota: I'd rather work in a regular restaurant because that way I'll learn how to cook.
Mariana: I hope you find a good job.
Kota: Thanks.

B *Replace the underlined words with your own information. Be sure to listen to your partner and change the underlined parts appropriately.*

DL 093　CD2-32　　　　DL 094　CD2-33

C *Listen to the rest of the conversation and answer the questions.*

1. What kind of job does Kota want to get after graduation?

2. What languages does Mariana speak?

3. What kind of job does Mariana want to get after graduation?

4. What is Kota going to do next month?

5. What were they doing towards the end of the conversation?

6. How do you say "thank you" in Portuguese?

75

EXPRESSIONS FOR INTERACTION

A *Practice each dialogue with a partner. Replace the underlined words with your own information.*

Expressing Intentions

1. A: **What are you going to do** after <u>you graduate</u>?
   B: **I'd like to** be <u>a tour guide</u> after <u>I graduate</u>.
   A: That sounds <u>like fun</u>. Good luck.

2. A: **What are you doing** <u>this weekend</u>?
   B: **I'm planning to** <u>go to the movies</u> with <u>my friends</u>.

Talking about Future Plans

1. A: **What are you going to do** <u>this summer</u>?
   B: **I'm thinking about** <u>volunteering</u> in <u>Thailand</u>.

2. A: **What's your plan for** <u>the future</u>?
   B: **I don't know, but I'd like to** <u>work overseas</u>.

B *Take turns asking a partner his/her plans for the future. Write your partner's plan on the lines provided.*

Example after this class

A: What are you doing after this class?
B: I have to work until 11:00.
A: Sorry to hear that. I thought we could have dinner together.
B: Thank you. Maybe next time.

Future time	Your partner's plan
1. this evening	_____
2. this Friday afternoon	_____
3. in the summer of your senior year	_____
4. when you turn 30	_____
5. when you turn 40	_____

C *Make a life plan. Take turns asking and answering the questions below. Use the expressions from the box. Be sure to give comments.*

Future plans	Responses
I'm going to …	Wow! Really?
I'm thinking about …	That sounds good.
I'm planning to …	That's great! Good luck!
How about you?	Are you serious?

1. What are you going to do after graduation?
2. Would you like to get married? If so, how many children do you want to have?
3. Where would you like to live?
4. Where would you like to travel in Japan … and overseas?
5. When would you like to retire?
6. What would you like to do during retirement?
7. *(Your own question)* _____?

WORLD ENGLISHES

Adjust your English

In international communication, you have to adjust the level, style, expressions you use, and other features of your English so that the English speakers you encounter can understand you and communicate with you comfortably. Of course the speakers you talk to must do the same. <u>Mutual adjustment</u> are the keywords here.

How can you simplify the following sentences in case your friends have trouble understanding you? Ask for help from your teacher if needed.

1. Hit me up when you are in town. ⇒ Give me a _____ when you come to town.
2. I got some chokkie and bikkies from a cabbie. ⇒ I got some _____ and biscuits from a _____ driver. (Australian)
3. We seek meager accommodations. ⇒ We want a _____ that is very cheap.
4. You need to clarify the nature of a flexible workforce. ⇒ (simplify)
_____

LISTENING ACTIVITIES

DL 096   CD2-35

Listen to the interview. Take notes and answer the questions.

Notes

....
....
....

Questions

1. Where in Brazil is this person from?
2. Why is she in Japan?
3. What is she planning on doing when she graduates?
4. What kind of job would she like to get?
5. Where would she like to work? Why?

READING ACTIVITIES

DL 097   CD2-36

Read the passage about unique jobs from the past.

Over the years there have been some jobs that have become extinct. One of these jobs is the bowling alley pinsetter. A pinsetter's job was to set the pins at a bowling alley. They would also have to clear the pins that had fallen after the first ball was bowled, and return the ball to the bowler each time. When the automated pinsetter machine was invented, the job of pinsetter was no longer needed.

Before most people could afford to buy an alarm clock there was a job known as the knocker-up. This person's job was to wake people up so they could get to work on time. A knocker-up would knock on their clients' windows until they woke up. They would not leave the clients' windows until they were sure their clients were awake. If the client lived on the second floor of a building, a long stick to knock on the windows of higher floors was used.

Another job that used long sticks was the job of lamplighter. Before electricity, oil or gas was used in lamps to light the streets. The lamplighter would have to go around lighting the lamps as well as extinguishing them each day.

Unit 13 Part-time/Future Jobs

A *Discuss the following questions with a partner.*

1. What did pinsetters, knocker-ups, and lamplighters do?
2. If you had to choose one of these jobs, which one would you choose? Why?
3. Which job seems the most difficult? Why?
4. Do you know any other jobs that are extinct?

GLOBAL ACTIVATOR

A *What would you do in the work-related situations below? Ask a partner. Begin by asking "What would you do if … ?"*

> Example
>
> You find out your hours have been cut at work.
>
> You: **What would you do if** you found out that your hours at work had been cut?
>
> Partner: I would talk to the manager to see why my hours had been cut. Then I would try to get more hours.

1. Your boss tells that you can work in Canada and get paid more, but you can't come back for ten years or you can stay in Japan and get paid less.
2. You check your bank account and you find you didn't get paid as much as you should have.
3. You oversleep and know you are going to be late for work.
4. You are 45 years old and you hate your job.
5. You have a project to finish at work, but you are not going to finish on time.

B *(Optional) Discuss the following questions with your group.*

- What is the best job that somebody you know has? Why is it such a good job?
- What is the worst job that somebody you know has? Why is it such a bad job?
- Which of the following jobs would you choose?
    - A job that pays a lot of money, but is difficult. You will hate this job.
    - A job that does NOT pay much, but you will love this job.

Unit 14

Experiences

Functions

Asking for Help/Talking about Experiences

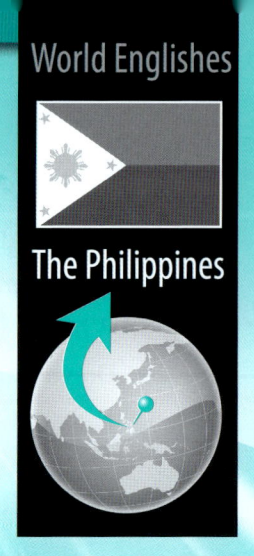

World Englishes

The Philippines

TOPIC QUESTIONS

A Fill in the blanks with your own information and practice saying them with a partner. Try to be original and informative.

1. *A:* What was the best thing that's ever happened to you?
   B: That would be when I _____.
   (met my girlfriend / entered this school)

2. *A:* What is the best place you've visited?
   B: The best place I've visited is _____.

3. *A:* Why was that place above so great?
   B: Because _____.
   (it was so beautiful / the people were so friendly there)

4. *A:* Have you ever done something you've really regretted?
   B: No, I haven't. / Yes, I've _____. (stolen my mom's money)

5. *A:* Have you ever lied about your _____? (age / weight / height)
   B: No, I haven't. / Yes, I lied about my _____ to _____ because _____.

6. *A:* What was a time when someone really helped you?
   B: It was when _____.
   (I was hit by a car / I didn't have enough money for rent)

B Change roles and ask the same questions. Be sure to ask and answer follow-up questions.

Unit 14 Experiences

DIALOGUE DL 098 · CD2-37 ● ▶ DL 099 · CD2-38

A *Listen to the conversation and practice with a partner.*

Atsuya is talking to Inday about his school project.

Atsuya: I'm wondering if you could help me with my paper.
Inday: Sure. How can I help?
Atsuya: I'd like to ask you about your experiences here in Japan.
Inday: Okay. You want to ask me now?
Atsuya: Yes. That is if you don't mind?
Inday: No, I don't mind at all. Go ahead.
Atsuya: Thank you. So, what has been your most difficult experience in Japan?
Inday: Finding an apartment. Many places wouldn't let me rent an apartment because I am not Japanese.
Atsuya: Oh, I'm sorry to hear that. How about your best experience?
Inday: Getting lost.
Atsuya: Getting lost?

B *Replace the underlined words with your own information. Be sure to listen to your partner and change the underlined parts appropriately.*

DL 100 · CD2-39 ● ▶ DL 101 · CD2-40

C *Listen to the rest of the conversation and fill in the blanks.*

1. Inday's best experience was getting lost because somebody _____ her to the place she wanted to go to.

2. Inday's favorite food is _____.

3. Inday wants Atsuya to take her to eat _____.

4. Inday has a _____ to attend after the interview.

5. Atsuya is interviewing Inday and a(n) _____ student as well as other international students in the _____ at five tomorrow.

EXPRESSIONS FOR INTERACTION

A *Practice each dialogue with a partner. Replace the underlined words with your own information.*

Asking for Help

1. *A:* **Would it be possible for you to** look at <u>my computer</u>?
   B: **Sure**, what's wrong with it?

2. *A:* **Do you think you could help me with** <u>my homework</u>?
   B: **No problem at all**.

Talking about Experiences

1. *A:* **What has been your** <u>most</u> <u>difficult</u> **experience** at school so far?
   B: **That would be** <u>attending nine o'clock classes</u>.

2. *A:* **Have you ever** met <u>a celebrity</u>?
   B: **Yes, in fact** I met <u>Sakurai Sho</u> on the way to school today.

B *Practice asking a partner politely for help by completing the conversations below. Your partner should politely accept or decline. Use the expressions below.*

Politely asking for help	Politely accepting or refusing help
• Would it be possible for you to … ? • Do you think you could … ? • I'm wondering if you could … ?	• I'd be glad to. How can I help you? • I'm sorry, but I can't. I have to … • I wish I could, but I …

1. I'm moving to a new apartment and need help. _____?
2. (in a restaurant) Oh, shoot! I left my wallet at home. _____?
3. I've run out of gas and I don't have a credit card with me. _____?
4. Oh, I missed my train and will be late for an important exam. _____?
5. I'm sorry but my foot is broken and I need help carrying my books to class. _____?

C *Respond to a partner's regrets with "You should/shouldn't have …" Then add one more sentence. The first one is done for you.*

1. A: I skipped my French class three times and the teacher said I've failed the class.
   B: Oh, you should've come to every class. He told us that we would fail if we cut classes three or more times. Don't you remember?

2. I played video games until 4:00 in the morning yesterday and I'm too sleepy now.
3. I had to pay almost 50,000 yen to fix my teeth at the dentist.
4. My eyesight is so bad now. I read too many comic books when I was little.
5. I didn't join the study abroad program last year and they said I couldn't join the program this year because I'm not a freshman.
6. I went out drinking with Yuka yesterday, and my girlfriend is so mad now that she said she would break up with me. What should I do?

DL 103 ~ 105   CD2-42 ~ CD2-44

WORLD ENGLISHES

How bad is really bad?

Pronunciation and grammar are important when speaking any language, but you can still make yourself understood with some mistakes. However, if it is too bad, people may have trouble understanding you.

Listen. Is their English good enough or do they need to work on it? Circle one.

A. unintelligible   understandable   not bad   pretty good   excellent
B. unintelligible   understandable   not bad   pretty good   excellent
C. unintelligible   understandable   not bad   pretty good   excellent

How can you improve the following sentences? Discuss with a partner or teacher.

1. I wanna shopping this weekend.
2. Our teacher can speak a lot of another country languages.
3. I did cospre in weekend and ate many chickens in the KFC.
4. I recommend movie is *Tonari no Totoro*.

LISTENING ACTIVITIES

DL 106　CD2-45

Listen to the interview. Take notes and answer the questions.

Notes

....
....
....

Questions

1. Where in the Philippines is this person from?
2. Why did she decide to come to Japan?
3. What is the best experience she's had in Japan?
4. What is the most difficult decision she's had to make?
5. What else did she say about her life in Japan?

READING ACTIVITIES

DL 107　CD2-46

Read the passage and fill in the blanks with the words listed below. Some words are used more than once.

| aboard | transportation | loud | knock | route |
| taxi | written | unique | waving | bus |

If you want a truly _____ experience when you visit the Philippines, then you should take a ride in a *jeepney*. A *jeepney* is like a small _____, which is known for its bright colors and _____ decorations. Each *jeepney* is also given a name that is usually _____ somewhere on the vehicle. Using this type of public _____ will give you a great experience while you are in the Philippines. A *jeepney* is similar to a _____ because it follows a certain route. When you see a *jeepney* there will be a person called a barker who yells out, or barks, the destinations the *jeepney* will go. It is also similar to a _____ because you can get off wherever

84

you want. However, the driver won't start the journey until there are enough people
_____. When you want the driver to stop, you simply _____ on the roof or say
para po, which means "please stop." The driver will stop anywhere on the _____
for you. If you see a *jeepney* on the street, you can also get him to stop by _____
your hand at him. Try this interesting mode of _____ if you ever find yourself in the
Philippines.

GLOBAL ACTIVATOR

A *Take turns asking the following questions with a partner to find out about each other's experiences. Make sure to take turns asking questions or giving comments to each other. The first one is done for you.*

1. A: What is the toughest decision you've ever had to make?
   B: The toughest decision I've ever had to make was whether I should tell my boyfriend how I felt about him.
   A: So, you said you liked him a lot. Then what happened?
   B: Well, you know the rest of the story. We're very happy now.

2. Have you ever been to a foreign country? If so, where did you go? How was it? (If not, where would you like to go? Why?)

3. What is the most dangerous situation you've ever been in? Tell me the story.

4. Have you ever done anything really, really bad? What was it?

5. Have you ever seen a ghost? Tell me the story. (If you have never seen a ghost, do you believe in ghosts? Why or why not?)

B *(Optional) In a small group, each person should talk about an interesting or surprising experience they've had. It can be a true experience or something they've made up. Guess whether their story is real or not.*

Unit 15

Cool Japan

World Englishes

France

Functions

Giving Suggestions/Opinions

TOPIC QUESTIONS

A *Fill in the blanks with your own information and practice saying them with a partner. Try to be original and informative.*

1. *A:* I'm thinking about teaching Japanese overseas. What do you think?
   B: I think it's a good/bad idea because you can _____.
       (live overseas / improve your foreign language skills …)

2. *A:* What do you think about cosplayers?
   B: I think _____.
       (they are fun / I'd like to become one / they are too strange …)

3. *A:* Should I work at a ramen restaurant or at a *juku*?
   B: You should work at _____ because _____.
       (you can make more money / it's more challenging than the other one …)

4. *A:* Please tell me your opinion about eating whale meat.
   B: Okay. I think _____.
       (we should stop it because … / it's okay because …)

5. *A:* Which martial art do you like better _____ or kendo?
       (karate / judo / aikido)
   B: I like _____ better because it _____.

6. *A:* My friend is visiting from _____. Can you suggest a cool place to take him?
   B: Yeah, you should take him to _____ because it is very, very Japanese.

B *Change roles and ask the same questions. Be sure to ask and answer follow-up questions.*

Unit 15 Cool Japan

💬 DIALOGUE 🎧 DL 108 CD2-47 ● 🎧 DL 109 CD2-48

A *Listen to the conversation and practice with a partner.*

Alain, a French student, is talking to Yuko about his parents' visit.

Yuko: How long will <u>your parents</u> be here?
Alain: For about <u>two weeks</u>. I'm not sure where I should take them.
Yuko: Are you planning on going to <u>Kyoto</u>?
Alain: Yes, they definitely want to go there.
Yuko: If you are going to be in <u>Kyoto</u>, then you should also visit <u>Nara</u>.
Alain: That's a good idea. I'm also thinking about <u>taking them to Osaka</u>. What should we do there?
Yuko: You should <u>eat *okonomiyaki* and *takoyaki*</u>.
Alain: That's a <u>good</u> idea. What else?
Yuko: Take them to <u>a pachinko parlor</u>.
Alain: What?

B *Replace the underlined words with your own information. Be sure to listen to your partner and change the underlined parts appropriately.*

🎧 DL 110 CD2-49 ● 🎧 DL 111 CD2-50

C *Listen to the rest of the conversation and fill in the chart.*

places to visit	what to see	what to eat
Osaka	aquarium	( )
( )	A-bomb dome ( ) Museum ( ) Museum	*okonomiyaki* and ( )
Miyajima in ( ) Prefecture	famous ( ) deer and monkeys	( )
( ) in ( ) Prefecture	Kintai Bridge	

EXPRESSIONS FOR INTERACTION

A *Practice each dialogue with a partner. Replace the underlined words with your own information.*

Giving Suggestions

1. A: **What should I** know before I go to Osaka?
   B: **You should** say *ookini* when you want to say "thank you."

2. A: **Do you have any idea about** where I should go in Tokyo?
   B: **Why don't you** go to Kaminarimon and the Tokyo Skytree?

Expressing Opinions

1. A: Kenji, when should we visit Japan?
   B: **Good question. You should** avoid June because it's the rainy season.

2. A: **I'm thinking about** studying in either Tokyo or Hiroshima.
   B: **It seems to me that** if you want to learn standard Japanese, Tokyo would be better, but it's also nice to learn some Hiroshima-*ben* in Hiroshima.

B *Work with a partner. A says what she/he is thinking about doing, using "I'm thinking about … ." B gives her/his opinion. Make sure B adds an extra comment.*

> **Example** buying a new car
> A: **I'm thinking about** buying a new car.
> B: **In my opinion, you should** buy a used car. They are a lot cheaper in Japan and probably run just fine.

1. becoming a manga artist but your drawing skills are not so good
2. taking your French friend to a public bath (a *sento*)
3. looking for a job as a maid waitress in a maid café in Tokyo
4. skipping your next class because you want to go to a cosplay festival right away
5. getting a traditional Japanese tattoo on your back

C *Work with a partner. Look at the situations on the next page. Take turns giving suggestions. Be sure to use "You should … ," "Why don't you … ?" or "If I were you, I would … ."*

Unit 15 Cool Japan

Example **Situation:** You burn your finger while cooking tempura.

A: I burned my finger while cooking tempura. **What should I do?**
B: **You should** put your finger under cool water.
A: Are you sure that'll work?
B: It's better than not doing anything.

1. You see your boyfriend/girlfriend on a date with another girl/boy.
2. Your friend's mother serves smelly *kusaya* and *hachinoko* when you are at their house.
3. When you told your French friend that no women are allowed on the sumo ring in Japan, she became angry and said that it was discrimination.
4. You are going to climb Mt. Fuji next summer.
5. You are thinking about learning how to play the *shakuhachi* but you can't find a teacher.

WORLD ENGLISHES

Use your emotions!

How you say something is often more important than what you say. A "yes" can sound like a "no" and "happy" can sound "sad" if you do not put the appropriate emotion into what you say.

Practice the dialogue with a partner two times with different emotions each time.

Marie: Pierre. I found a nice boyfriend. He is really handsome and sweet.
Pierre: Wow. That's wonderful. You got a boyfriend! What's the lucky man's name?

1st time: **really happy** (You know Marie was really sad when she broke up with her old boyfriend. So, you're so glad that she found a new boyfriend.)

2nd time: **really sad** (Actually you like Marie soooo much. You're now depressed that she found a boyfriend. You want to be her boyfriend.)

LISTENING ACTIVITIES

Listen to the interview. Take notes and answer the questions.

Notes

....
....
....

Questions

1. What brought him to Japan?
2. What Japanese dishes does he like?
3. What does he think is cool about Japan?
4. What does he think Japan should do to attract more international visitors?
5. Do you agree with him?

READING ACTIVITIES

Read the list of unique French laws below.

Many countries have strange laws that aren't always enforced, but some French laws seem to be really cool to Japanese. Here are some examples.

1. If you want to take your pet on the TGV, France's high-speed train, you need to buy it a ticket. This is also true for snails or any other domesticated animal even if it weighs under five kilograms.

2. There is a peculiar law in place for school cafeterias. It is illegal for students to have access to unlimited, self-serve ketchup, mayonnaise, or vinaigrette salad dressing in French school cafeterias. This law was made to encourage healthy eating habits among French children.

3. Part of the Toubon Law, which was passed in 1994, states that at least 40% of the music French radio stations play must be in French and half of that must be music from new musicians or productions. One of the reasons that this law was passed was to encourage the use and improvement of the French language.

4. It is legal to marry a dead person, but you have to show proof that you were planning on getting married before the other person died. In 1959 a dam burst and among the dead was a man who had planned to marry a woman. The woman was pregnant and she was so upset that a law was written to allow her to wed her deceased fiancé.

Unit 15 Cool Japan

A *Fill in the blanks with the appropriate words below.*

| young | alive | 5 | dead | 10 | self-serve | red | 40 | healthy |

Here are some really unique laws in France. Even animals that weigh under (　　　) kilograms need to have a ticket to ride on the TGV train. It is also illegal for students to have access to unlimited, (　　　) ketchup or mayonnaise at school. This is to encourage (　　　) eating habits among French children. There is also a law that states that at least (　　　) % of the music played on the radio must be in French to encourage the use of French language. Here is another cool law in France. You can marry a(n) (　　　) person in France if you were engaged to the person while he/she was (　　　).

GLOBAL ACTIVATOR

A *Imagine you have a group of international guests visiting you who want to taste, see, and experience "cool Japan." With a partner discuss what you both would recommend.*

> **Example** the coolest Japanese dishes
>
> A: **What do you think is** the coolest dish in Japan? Any idea on what they should eat?
> B: **I think they should** try tempura or sushi.
> A: **No, they should try** something they've never tried. How about *monja-yaki*?
> B: *Monja* **sounds good. And they should try** hot sake, you know, *atsukan*, too.
> A: **That would be very cool.**

1. the coolest place they should visit
2. the coolest experience they should have
3. the coolest thing they should buy
4. the coolest person they should meet
5. the coolest song they should listen to

B *(Optional)* In a small group, discuss what Japan should promote to attract more young international travelers. Try to introduce something really cool about Japan. Report back to the class.

Acknowledgment

We would like to thank the following speakers of World Englishes who helped us with the recordings in this book.

Anthony Beaucamp
Amanda Oyakawa
Amy Stotts
Bhakti Shah
Birgit Oguro
David Laurence
Demetre Evans
Erika Hernandez
Fatin Azahari
Gareth Thomas
Gregory King
Huang Wenjie
Ito Fuko
Jessica Nakagawa
Joshua Skookum
Joung Hee Krzic
Kashima Takashi
Kobayashi Ryusei
Lam Kan Yan
Ma. Estrella Luz Peñaloza
Nagae Kanto
Nakashima Yuka
Nemoto Reiju
Otsubo Chika
Pat Maher
Shiozawa Tadashi
Sugiyama Yuta
Wang Qian
Yuko King

本書には音声CD（別売）があります

Global Activator
Your English, My English, World Englishes!
大学生のためのグローバル時代の英会話

2015 年 1 月 20 日　初版第 1 刷発行
2025 年 2 月 20 日　初版第 17 刷発行

著　者　　塩　澤　　正
　　　　　Gregory A. King

発行者　　福　岡　正　人
発行所　　株式会社　金　星　堂
（〒101-0051）東京都千代田区神田神保町 3-21
Tel. (03) 3263-3828（営業部）
(03) 3263-3997（編集部）
Fax (03) 3263-0716
https://www.kinsei-do.co.jp

編集担当　今門貴浩　　　　　　　Printed in Japan
印刷所／日新印刷株式会社　製本所／松島製本
本書の無断複製・複写は著作権法上での例外を除き禁じられています。本書を代行業者等の第三者に依頼してスキャンやデジタル化することは、たとえ個人や家庭内での利用であっても認められておりません。
落丁・乱丁本はお取り替えいたします。
ISBN978-4-7647-4003-7　C1082